*Routledge Revivals*

# THE BOOKBINDING CRAFT AND INDUSTRY

# THE BOOKBINDING CRAFT AND INDUSTRY

## AN OUTLINE OF ITS HISTORY, DEVELOPMENT AND TECHNIQUE

BY

**T. HARRISON**

SECOND EDITION

Routledge
Taylor & Francis Group

First published by Sir Isaac Pitman and Sons, Ltd

This edition first published in 2018 by Routledge
2 Park Square, Milton Park, Abingdon, Oxon, OX14 4RN
and by Routledge
52 Vanderbilt Avenue, New York, NY 10017, USA

*Routledge is an imprint of the Taylor & Francis Group, an informa business*



**Publisher's Note**
The publisher has gone to great lengths to ensure the quality of this reprint but points out that some imperfections in the original copies may be apparent.

**Disclaimer**
The publisher has made every effort to trace copyright holders and welcomes correspondence from those they have been unable to contact.

A Library of Congress record exists under ISBN: 83048234

ISBN 13: 978-0-367-13897-4 (hbk)
ISBN 13: 978-0-367-13899-8 (pbk)
ISBN 13: 978-0-429-02910-3 (ebk)

KNIGHTS & COTTRELL
6A TUDOR ST LONDON EC
TELEGRAMS "CHALCOGRAPHERS" LONDON
DESIGNING AND ENGRAVING FOR PUBLISHERS AND BOOKBINDERS
TELEPHONE: CENTRAL 6162

# THE BOOKBINDING CRAFT AND INDUSTRY

" CLOSE-UP " VIEWS OF BOOKBINDING MACHINES IN OPERATION

1. The Brehmer Sewer.
2. 32-page Book Folder.
3. Three-side Book Trimmer.
4. The Rounding and Backing Machine.
5. Hydraulic Presses.
6. Smyth Sewing Machine.

[*Frontispiece*

PITMAN'S COMMON COMMODITIES AND INDUSTRIES SERIES

# THE BOOKBINDING CRAFT AND INDUSTRY

## AN OUTLINE OF ITS HISTORY, DEVELOPMENT AND TECHNIQUE

BY

T. HARRISON

CITY AND GUILDS OF LONDON SILVER AND BRONZE MEDALLIST
FORMERLY INSTRUCTOR IN BOOKBINDING AND DESIGN
SCIENCE AND ARTS FULL TECHNOLOGICAL CERTIFICATE

*SECOND EDITION*

LONDON
SIR ISAAC PITMAN & SONS, LTD.
PARKER STREET, KINGSWAY, W.C.2
BATH, MELBOURNE, TORONTO, NEW YORK

PRINTED IN GREAT BRITAIN
AT THE PITMAN PRESS, BATH

# PREFACE

WITHIN the scope of so small a book, it would be impossible to do other than skim the surface of a subject so full of historic interest, so varied, and so very controversial as that of Bookbinding. Although it is to be hoped that the technical aspect may be interesting and helpful to many fellow craftsmen, this cannot claim to be a complete technical work. The subject matter has been mainly designed to arouse the interest of the general reader, to be of utility to the librarian and bookseller, and of value to the bibliophile.

There are few crafts practised to-day that can claim such antiquity as the craft of bookbinding and yet, in its sounder principles, it is so little known.

It may appear futile in these days of mass production to deal with a hand craft at all ; but behind the plan of this work, there has always been the intention of examining the foundation principles which have so thoroughly stood the test of time, in the hope that in the development of mechanical production, these principles may not be overlooked.

T. H.

18 FLEETWOOD ROAD,
LONDON, N.W.10.

# CONTENTS

# ILLUSTRATIONS

GENERAL VIEW OF A MODERN BINDERY

THE

# BOOKBINDING CRAFT AND INDUSTRY

## CHAPTER I

### THE EVOLUTION OF THE BOOK

ENTHUSIASTIC antiquaries amongst bookbinders are insistent in claiming that their craft dates back to the time when the Assyrians and Babylonians used tablets of clay for keeping their records. These tablets, which had their characters impressed on the surface, were baked to make them hard, and then protected with an outer covering also of clay, in the form of an envelope. As it is generally admitted that the work of a bookbinder consists largely of covering and protecting records, their claim is somewhat justified, although the relationship is about as far distant as the date.

In the later development of Roman times, records were kept on wax tablets, which were made by the hollowing out of wooden panels and filling the hollow with wax. The characters were then marked on the surface with a point which was called a style. There were generally two tablets connected together with rings and consequently given the name of diptych, meaning twofold. It did not, however, necessarily follow that they were always in twos, as they were occasionally joined in series of three or more.

The joining together of these tablets may justly be claimed as bookbinding, of a nature which is to-day considered of utility in binding sketch-books, albums, and the like. Even the ultra-modern looseleaf system is not a very far cry from the ancient Roman diptych.

The Egyptians found a way of making flat leaves from the papyrus reed on which they scratched their wonderful hieroglyphics, obviously so full of meaning. The very word papyrus seems, in spite of its antiquity, to bring us closely in touch with that ancient and wonderful people when we consider what the word paper means to us to-day.

Although paper as we know it has no direct relationship with the papyrus, there is a close relationship in character, and to the binder a direct relationship between the method of holding these leaves together, and many of the commercial methods of modern times. When we fix together at the corners a number of typewritten sheets, in whatever method we may choose to adopt, we are only doing what the Egyptians did long before the Christian era; and when we carry the means of attachment down the sides, as we do in the case of magazines and similar productions, we are still not very far removed from those ancient methods of attachment.

In the evolution of the book as we know it to-day, its development may be traced from two distinct sources. First from the eastern scrolls, and second from the folded and insetted Roman vellum leaves. The oriental

scrolls were continuous rolls many feet in length and had the characters written across, so that the scroll was rolled at the one end and unrolled at the other in the course of its perusal.

Occasionally they were written lengthwise along the scroll, when no doubt the inconvenience of rolling and unrolling for each line led first to their being divided into columns, and eventually to the folding of the scroll between the columns zigzag fashion, and so forming a closer resemblance to our modern book with

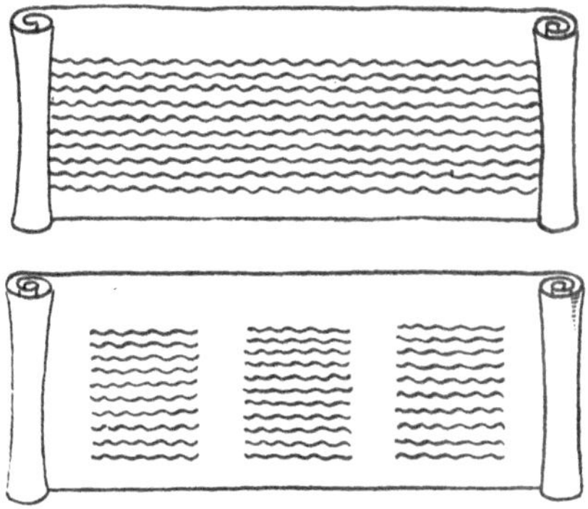

ROLLED SCROLLS

FOLDED ZIGZAG SCROLL

its series of leaves folded in the back. It requires very little imagination to see the desirability of joining up these folds at the back, thus enabling the leaves to be turned over without fear of displacement. Even at the present day, a method similar in construction to that of the folded scroll is adopted by the Chinese and Japanese, primarily because of the fineness and transparency of the paper used, and the undesirability of using both sides of the leaves.

Later, the idea of economy possibly suggested to the Egyptians and their neighbours the desirability of slitting the front fold of the zigzag leaf and utilizing both sides of the page. This opening of the fold at the front and fixing together the back folds would soon suggest the need for more strength; the leaves were therefore insetted the one into the other, thus enabling them to be stitched together, and so the book consisting of sections arrived.

Farther west new mediums had been discovered on which records could be made, viz. parchment and vellum. Their speedy development was probably due to the restriction placed on the exportation of papyrus from Egypt. Vellum was made from the skins of calves, and parchment from sheep skins. The leaves were cut double the required size, and these folded leaves were insetted and stitched through the middle. When the sections became unwieldy in thickness, it was a simple matter to make a series of smaller sections, leaving the ends of the threads to be tied, so forming a complete book made of a series of sections bound together.

The desirability of more strength naturally suggested that the ends of the threads could be better utilized by fixing them round the cords, thus joining the sections more effectually, especially as the loose ends of the cord supplied a means of attaching protecting boards.

Paper had probably been used in China many centuries before its introduction into Persia, and in the Asiatic countries it was known for many centuries before it came into general use in Europe. The introduction of printing made its use an absolute necessity, but the single-folded leaf with others insetted remained for a time. Once a second fold was introduced, making a quarto book, it was only a matter of further multiples to arrive at the huge printed sheets of to-day, consisting of as many as sixty-four page sections.

The evolution of the book through all its phases having been outlined, the modern printed sheet and its method of folding may now be considered.

# CHAPTER II

## FOLDING

PAPER is made in many sizes and to each of these a name is given. To give the whole of these sizes in detail would almost be impracticable, for the modern tendency is to ignore or modify the old standard of sizes to the utter bewilderment of those concerned in handling paper. The more generally accepted sizes for bookwork are—

| | |
|---|---|
| Crown . . . | 20 in. × 15 in. |
| Demy . . . | 22½ in. × 17½ in. |
| Royal . . . | 25 in. × 20 in. |
| Imperial . . . | 30 in. × 22 in. |

With the development of large printing presses the paper is made in double sizes and so we get: Double Imperial, Double Crown, etc. They go farther than this even and make some quadruple, giving the names of Quad. Crown, etc. While we ignore for the nonce the double and quadruple, our attention should be kept on the standard single sizes so as to understand more readily the names of the various book sizes.

It may be justly claimed that these sizes are misleading in so far that they may be made up from paper of any measurement, or the book may be so cut down that the size cannot be identified. The old standard sizes, however, still remain as a general guide, although a so-called octavo book may be in reality a 16mo. The origin of these accepted names may assist in the elucidation. When a full-sized sheet is folded once, it is called a Folio and written 2o. If the sheet is Imperial, it is called Imperial 2o. Crown 2o when crown size is used, etc. As an indication of the ebbing significance of these names the number of pages is often given instead of the usual sizes, as Four pages Imperial, i.e. 4 pp. Imp. As in the original form of the folded leaf, the folio is rarely made up without insetting even to-day. Should the sheet be folded a second time, it is termed a Quarto and written thus, 4to, being four leaves or eight pages. The name of the sheet is prefixed as before : Imp. 4to or 8 pp. Imp., etc. Another fold doubles the number of leaves and so we get Octavo (8vo) with the original size prefixed, or the newer method 16 pp. Imp., etc. A further fold gives us 16mo or 32 pp. Imp., and yet another brings us to 32mo or 64 pp.

A 12mo or 24mo is folded into a third instead of half in the first or second folds, and an 18mo is folded into a third, twice ; as the multiple indicates. Whatever the previous folds may have been, the final is always a straightforward double ensuring each leaf's going round the back, thus enabling all to be secured in the subsequent sewing.

The binder has no choice in the layout of the book. The printer has determined that for him and not always to its advantage. It is sometimes necessary to fold over a portion of the book and cut it away, then to fold each portion separately and to insert the one into the other ; but, whatever form the folding may take, the size is taken from the number of leaves in each section.

It is the duty of the binder to bind up a book after the printer has determined, not only the type and lay-out, but the paper also ; it is to be regretted that the printer does not always consider the final aspect of his book and select a paper that is suitable for binding. Too often, he is satisfied if his type looks well on the paper, in disregard of the fact that the paper may not bend properly when being bound up.

It is frequently found that a 12mo book printed on stiff, coarse paper will open only with difficulty and never properly close again after being opened. Paper that may be eminently suitable for a folio may be quite a failure when used for a 12mo and vice versa. Paper for binding should bend readily without breaking and its flexibility be considered in relation to its size.

In machine-made papers whenever practicable, the fibres, which run all one way, should be so folded as to go right across the back to obtain the maximum of strength. In hand-made papers the fibres run in all directions, so this fact has less bearing on them. The thickness of the sections should also be considered, as it is impossible to make a successful binding of a book when the sections are too thick, and, if they are too thin, it is equally impossible to obtain a strong binding without resorting to methods which are not always acceptable.

Considering the methods of folding, it is always necessary to analyse the layout of the sheets as they come from the printer. A printer may determine the succession of his paging by first folding a sheet to the size he desires, and then cutting out a V-shape in the middle of the section so that it pierces each sheet. It is simple for him to lift up the corner of each V-shaped piece, and number it in proper succession. When the sheet is opened out again, the layout of his sheet is determined for him, but when the book gets into the binder's hands he has to discover for himself how the sheet was originally folded. This can be determined by observing that the numbers of the opposing leaves are in succession when folded over.

Each sheet generally has what is known as a signature, or identification mark, which is to be found usually at the bottom of the first page of each section, either at the right, or at the left-hand side, or in the middle. These signatures usually take the form of letters of the alphabet, the letters J, V, and W being omitted. Apparently, these omissions are a survival of the days when books were mostly printed in Latin and these letters had no separate identities. This rule is not altogether invariable, and the pagination should be examined to be sure that these omissions are intentional.

The general text of the book usually starts with the letter B, the title, etc., being considered as A. If the preliminary matter runs into several sheets, the signatures for these are often given in small letters, or "lower case," as the printer would say. The preliminary matter, however, rarely exceeds one sheet; but, when it does, the small alphabet is continued up to the beginning of the text. Then the capital or "upper case" letters start where the book proper begins, and continue until the alphabet is exhausted, when a new start is made if necessary with AA and onwards to the end of the alphabet; and, if the book is a very thick one, AAA and onwards may be necessary. Variations of this form of continuance of the second and third alphabets are in use such as a capital and a small letter together, Aa, Aaa, or 2A, 2B, etc., and the third alphabet 3A, 3B, and so on. Figures are sometimes used, and these, of course, follow on consecutively to the end. Sometimes a figure will be seen to follow the letter, as 2B3. The 2 marks the second alphabet, the B indicates the second sheet of the second alphabet, and the 3 following is generally the third leaf of that particular section, or it may be an indication that the portion so marked is an inset of the sheet.

When sheets are printed in duplicate, both sides of the paper are set up together, and when they are pulled off the sheet is turned over on the machine in such a way as to impress the opposite sides and thus give a double printed sheet with a single setting. These sheets are cut in two by the binder before he proceeds to fold them.

The folding is the first operation the modern binder has to consider, and, if the books are supplied in large quantities from the printer, each signature will be in a separate parcel and the peculiarities of each sheet will first be noted by making up a sample copy. The making up of the sample volume has many advantages, chief amongst them being the fact that pitfalls may be discovered and so avoided in the bulk ; and also a book completed in all its processes enables the cases for the final operation to be made ready whilst the folding is proceeding. If books are supplied in flat sheets, in single copies, or small quantities, they will probably have been gathered into separate books from the stock sheets and supplied in that form. This is spoken of as book folding as distinct from sheet folding, and has a direct bearing on the cost, as, in folding some thousands of sheets of the same signature, the operator, having discovered the peculiarities or " set " as it is called of the sheet, is able to get up speed in a way that is not possible when the set of each sheet has to be discovered in rotation.

The sheets to be folded lie out on the bench lengthwise in piles of about 500, the signature being on the left-hand side nearest the operator and on the underneath side. A few of the top leaves are gripped between the thumb and first finger, and bent over in such a way as to make them project one beyond the other in a minute degree. This is known as " fanning out," and has for object the handling of each single leaf with sureness and expedition.

The tool used for folding is made of bone, about

8 in. or 9 in. long and 1 in. wide, both edges shaped like a very blunt knife ; this is called a " folder." The folder is held in the right hand while the sheet is drawn over with the left from right to left side without creasing the paper ; the print of the two pages thus facing each other must exactly register. This is assured by the operator's laying the point of the folder on the pagination mark, lifting up the sheet to that point and moving it until the two pages are in perfect registration, then holding the sheet perfectly square with the left hand, the first fold is creased by drawing the edge of the folder

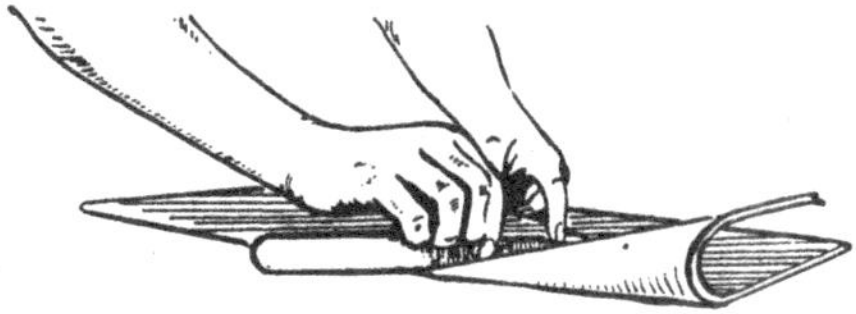

HAND-FOLDING

over the fold, from the middle away from the operator, then bringing it down the sheet towards the operator and so making a perfect crease in the paper. For the next fold the sheet is held in the middle of the first fold by the folder and with the left hand the top right-hand corner is drawn over until the pagination of the opposing sheets registers, and the crease is completed by running the folder off the top right-hand corner along to the left. The next fold is taken at right angles to the operator and is merely a repetition of the previous operations.

The printing being assumed to be in perfect register, if the folded sheet is pricked with a pin through the pagination of the top leaf, the hole should go through the pagination in all the leaves.

If any error has been made in the folding, the succession of the pagination will at once make this apparent.

It will be observed that in many thick papers an unsightly crease will make its appearance, radiating from the folded corner at the back. This may be avoided by cutting the fold of the sheet a little beyond the half-way point before the next fold is made. This adds to the cost of the folding; but is well worth the extra cost for good work. It is sometimes only necessary

*By courtesy of Messrs. Smyth-Horne, Ltd.*

THE CHAMBERS PAPER-FOLDING MACHINE

to cut at the second, or sometimes only at the third fold to be effective.

The folded edges of the paper that must eventually be cut to open into the pages are referred to as the "bolts." These will be opened by the subsequent cutting of the edges.

The description of the folding given is that of a 16-page or octavo sheet. All other forms are similar in technique, the only precaution necessary being to take note of the divisions into thirds and other multiples, and the likelihood of insets. As before stated, the signature appears on the front page of the folded sheets, and these sheets are laid in regular piles to the left hand with the signature facing upwards and the front edges towards the operator.

There are many machines on the market for this process, and the speed at which the sheets are folded is truly remarkable. These machines are suitable only for long runs of work, as a certain amount of time is taken up in setting them for individual sheets. The register in machine-folding is obtained by setting the sheets to the edge of the paper, a point that has to be taken into consideration by the printer in the first instance, if accurate registration is to result.

# CHAPTER III

## GATHERING, COLLATING, AND PULLING

WHEN all the sheets of a book have been folded, they are stacked in piles of individual signatures in proper sequence, on a long table. They are then gathered by taking one section from each pile in the order as placed. Thus as the operator walks along the table taking one section from the succession of piles, a book has been completed at the end of the table. This process is referred to as " gathering."

Economy of time is effected by using both sides of a table, so that on the return journey a second book can be gathered ; this is more usual when more than one operator is at work on the same series of sheets. If the gathering is done single-handed, two piles are made, the one behind the other, and on returning the sheets gathered from the second series ; or if space is limited, it is usual to work the series half-way through to the front of the table, and the remainder behind, so that the book is completed when the operator has returned to where the start was made. A circular table may be used with effect, and if a table is made to revolve a series of operators may sit and gather the sheets as they pass. As the human operator has not yet developed into a machine, this method in practice is fraught with too many possibilities of inaccuracies for it to be very popular. There are very elaborate and complicated machines for this process which do the work both quickly and accurately.

To ensure accuracy a check is usually made to each completed book. This is known as " collating," and is done by gripping the book with the right hand firmly in the right-hand top corner with the fingers downwards, and by giving the wrist a twist she will fan out the sections; then lightly holding the opposite corner in the left hand, she can release the folded backs one at a time with the thumb; and, as they are released, they will spring back sufficiently to allow each signature to be

*By courtesy of* *The T. W. & C. B. Sheridan Co. Ltd.*

GATHERING AND BINDING MACHINE WHICH WORKS AT THE RATE OF 7,800 BOOKS PER HOUR

seen, and the sequence to be properly checked ready for the next process to be undertaken.

In some books the printer will put a small black mark on each sheet to appear on the edge of the outside fold, and on each successive sheet this mark is placed at a regular distance below the preceding one, giving a diagonal line across the back of the book when gathered. If any one sheet is out of place or missing, it is apparent at once by the diagonal lines being broken, and so saves the process of individual collating.

So far only straightforward edition work has been dealt with, and it is now necessary to call a halt and consider the treatment of miscellaneous or "old work" as it is called: old books that require rebinding, new books that have been issued in temporary paper covers, and cloth books for which the purchaser desires stronger and more permanent binding than that given in the edition workshops.

The majority of books issued in this country are sent out from the publishers in semi-permanent cloth cases, quite suitable for most people, but not strong enough for libraries, and not good enough for those whose tastes and circumstances call for beautiful and substantial binding. On the Continent a large number of books are issued in paper covers which necessitate a proper binding if it be intended to preserve them at all. So, for rebinding, a book must be brought back to the condition in which we left the collated copies of edition work.

For a miscellaneous binder of repute to bind up a book imperfect is an unpardonable sin; so it is very unwise for a binder to interfere with a book until he is sure that it is perfect, as such an action may recoil on his reputation and lay him open to serious charges. This being the case, it is a matter of expediency that the book be paged and the plates checked off as soon as it is received, before anything else is done with it. Plates, of course, do not page in with the book as a general rule.

The preliminary matter is usually paged in Roman numerals, but several of the early pages do not have a pagination mark at all, so it is necessary to count back from the first numbered page. This is a vital and necessary check, as it may be the only indication of a missing half-title, and half-titles have a happy knack of going astray, and in rare books this may knock pounds off the value of the book.

Preliminary matter, then, consists usually of a half-title, frontispiece, title, dedication, contents, list of illustrations, preface, and introduction. The pagination may not begin until the contents sheet is reached, or it may even start as far on as the preface ; but, with rare exceptions, it takes the preceding pages into consideration. So the frontispiece being assumed to be a separate plate and not part of the section, and the dedication, contents, and list of illustrations to take up one leaf each, the preface would start the Roman numerals with XI, and from thence onward the checking is simple and straightforward.

Imperfections discovered are indicated by putting in what is known as a " peg." This is simply a strip of paper laid in the place of the damaged or missing leaf and projecting beyond the edge, and is looked upon as a danger signal. All imperfections are reported to the owner and records of such reports kept for subsequent protection should the owner decide on having the book bound imperfect.

Very old books may have no pagination, and frequently those that have cannot be relied upon as being correct, as it is not at all unusual to find for instance, number 19 on one side of the page and number 26 printed overleaf ; and other glaring errors of a similar nature. A fairly good indication of the sequence, however, may be found in the " tag " or catchword at the bottom of each page, which is merely a repetition of the first word on the following page. For some old and rare books a complete knowledge of the history of the particular book is the only means of being certain that it is perfect.

The pagination of some old books is so erratic that

many binders keep elaborate records of their peculiarities for future guidance, while many can be checked only from existing copies known to be perfect, and the British Museum is much used for this purpose. Experts who specialize in this work, and owners of rare books, usually know the condition of every leaf before the book gets into the binder's hands.

Assuming the book to be perfect, the binder proceeds to take it to pieces. This is known as "pulling," and may require extreme care and judgment. The easiest books to pull are those issued in paper covers, the sections being "French" sewn like the bulk of Continental books; they are held together in the simplest possible way and can therefore be pulled with the minimum risk of injury to the book. The whole construction of a book largely depends on the condition of the fold at the back of the section, from which it is built up, so that it is necessary to exercise care in the pulling, which must be done firmly and with decision. There is one other point to be considered; books issued in paper covers frequently have their wrappers bound in with them. From the collector's point of view the book is then bound in its entirety which may add materially to its value at some future date. It may be that the covers are placed just as issued, or they may be placed at the end. Occasionally they are bound in for their artistic merit, and may be quite a feature of the book; sometimes they are not bound in owing to their lack of merit, artistic or otherwise; and consequently much satisfaction is derived from tearing them off and consigning them to a place where they will cease to offend artistic sensibilities.

The question of the covers having been decided, the construction of the first section must now be taken into consideration to find out how it is made up, care being taken to preserve any blank leaves which may form part of the section. The middle of the first section is found by opening up the back until the thread is seen. This thread is cut in as many places as it pierces the section. Then, noting the number of leaves that go to the first half of the section, the puller counts the same number to the second half of the section, when to verify its accuracy the signature of the following sheet should be apparent. All doubts being removed, the right hand is laid firmly on the book, and with the left the section is pulled away from the rest of the book and laid at the left-hand side of the operator, after having removed any glue or paper that may adhere to the back. This can usually be pulled off with the fingers, but sometimes it is necessary to use a blunt knife for the purpose, bending the back of the section in such a way that it will face upwards when laid on the table, and a careful flick of the knife will remove it. Any misjudgment in the division of the sections will result in two single leaves requiring more time to patch together than was taken to pull them apart ; and failure to cut the threads will result in the whole section's being in single leaves, or, as nearly as makes no matter, when the subsequent sewing has to be considered.

After the first sheet is pulled, the construction of the next is noted to see if it is 2, 4, 6, or more leaves to the centre, after which it is fairly safe to take it as the basis for the rest of the book.

In the case of the majority of these paper-wrappered books the sewing is of the flimsiest, and the book almost falls to pieces once the threads are cut ; and the glue, whether by design or otherwise, simply shells off, leaving the book quite uninjured—a point in favour of continental publications in the permanent binder's eyes.

The next form of book to be considered for pulling is the cloth-cased book, so favoured by English and American publishers. As a preliminary to pulling this, it is usual to open and bend the book right back on itself in a number of places to release some of the glue on the back and enable the operator to open more readily into the back of the sections for cutting the threads. The judicious releasing of the end paper and cover next calls for attention. The end paper will have been tipped with paste on to the half-title, so by holding the book firmly in the right hand, and gripping the end paper and cover together with the left, the tipped portion of the end paper will yield when the hands are drawn apart, coming away with the cover. When two papers are tipped together and require separating, this can be done more readily if one of the leaves can be sacrificed. By keeping the one to be preserved flat and rigid and the other bent well over, it will be found when they are separated that the bent one has left a portion of itself adhering to the rigid one, and the rigid one, although sound, still bears a disfiguring reminder of its previous companion. It is frequently a choice of evils of which the latter is the lesser.

This fact is apparent when the end paper is separated from the book. This separation will disclose a strip of mull or linen which has been glued on to the back of the book and then fastened between the cover and the end paper. This is cut through with a sharp knife at both ends of the book and the cloth case will then fall away. The back of the book now being exposed, as much of the lining as will readily come away is removed, making it easier for the operator to pull the book.

The same mode of procedure is followed out as in the case of the paper-wrappered book, but greater care is necessary in removing the glue and lining from the edges of the sections; the cloth-bound book, having been bound with an idea of more or less permanency, is therefore more securely put together, and consequently more difficult to take apart.

In dealing with hand-sewn leather-bound books, even greater care is needed, as the stronger binding adds to the difficulty of pulling, and increases the risks of injuring the sections. Occasionally, when the cover has rotted away leaving the sewing firm and sound, it is inadvisable to pull and re-sew; but better to be content with re-covering only. In very old books it was the custom to bake the glue hard on the back, and cover with the leather fast to the back of the book. If the perishing of the threads makes the pulling of such a book necessary, it is usual to soak off the glue and pull while the back of the book is still moist. As much of the leather as is possible is pulled off, then the whole of the back is covered with a layer of thick paste and allowed to stand for four or five hours, and sometimes the application of more paste is necessary from time to time. While the back is soaking it is better to keep the book nice and firm in the press. The surplus paste is next scraped off and the back finally washed with warm water to remove as much glue as possible, then the book is pulled whilst still wet; as, the soaking having driven the glue farther into the back, it would not separate readily if allowed to dry.

When separated the sections have to be laid in such a way as to prevent the still damp sticky ridge along the back from sticking to anything it lies on, especially its companion section. This can be done by laying the backs opposite ways alternately, so that the moist edges are suspended.

# CHAPTER IV

## PREPARATION OF MISCELLANEOUS WORK

If the modern binder's work consisted of binding together only well constructed sections, his task would be fairly simple. Among the many problems to be faced is the binding together successfully of volumes consisting of single leaves; manuscript and typescripts often come within this category. These may at times be made up in the back so as to form sections; for example :—folios 1 and 4 may be joined together, then folios 2 and 3 joined and inserted; 6 or more, even numbers may be joined to make up a section according to the nature and thickness of the paper. This will present one difficulty which becomes increasingly awkward. As the thickness of the book is increased, the joinings of the paper together in the back giving added thickness to each sheet, may double the thickness at the back compared with the fore-edge. This can be overcome in some instances by paring away the joined edges of the paper, but it is a costly process and not always practicable. The bulk may be minimized by beating down the edges before joining, and excessive pressing afterwards. This method is only possible with soft papers that will yield to pressure, as hard papers would crack and break under such treatment, resulting in weakness where strength is needed.

A thin Japanese paper is sometimes used reducing the bulk to a minimum; but the strength in the fold is only sufficient to carry light leaves and small books. This method is very useful in the case of old books where the back is too perished to bind without strengthening, and yet too valuable to have any of it cut away, Japanese tissue being the strongest medium possible for comparative bulk.

In many cases, however, single leaves are made into sections by overcasting, or whipstitching as it is called in some parts of the country.

For overcasting it is first necessary to knock up the back of the leaves perfectly flush, with the head of the book kept quite square, then across, the back at a convenient point near the head and tail, a tip of thin glue is given, sufficient to hold the leaves together temporarily, and when dry the book is separated into convenient sections. Each section is then laid flat on the bench, the edge to be overcast projecting slightly to allow the needle to go through clear of the edge of the bench. Assuming the book to be an octavo, the first stitch is made at a distance of a quarter of an inch from the tail, and a full eighth of an inch from the back, working downwards. The thread is then drawn through, and the end knotted ; the needle is passed down again into the same hole, brought through from underneath over the back edge, piercing the upper side again at a distance of about half an inch from the last stitch, working at regular intervals towards the head of the book, where the thread is finally knotted and cut, leaving the overcasted section complete. After treating the whole of the book in this manner it is more or less in the position of a book composed of folded sections, and is now ready for sewing.

There are many objections raised to this method ; but if treated properly in subsequent processes, it answers most practical purposes admirably. Other methods of treating single leaves deal more with the handling in bulk rather than sections, and really come under the heading of sewing.

The handling of plates is often a matter of grave concern and difficulty for the binder. In the original make-up of the book the text matter is planned, and the plates simply inserted in their proper places according to the text, and it sometimes happens that the weight and bulk of the plates are in excess of that of the section in which they are generally tipped. This is unreasonable from the binder's point of view, and might easily have been avoided by a little forethought, by arranging at least some of the plates to fold across the sections ; and also by reducing the original size of the sections where there is a preponderance of plates.

It is the binder's business, however, to make the best of the book as it is, irrespective of previous arrangement ; but this lack of foresight adds materially to the cost of the binding, and at best, only results in a makeshift job.

The generally accepted method of attaching plates is to fan out a dozen or more, and tip with paste to the width of from an eighth to a quarter of an inch or more, according to size, substance, and nature of the paper. The pasting is done on the back of the plate and the plates are placed well into the back and allowed to dry under a weight.

Plates are sometimes supplied larger than the book, and in that case it is an advantage, if the cost admits of it, to allow say, a quarter of an inch when cutting, to turn round the section to which it belongs ; this makes a stronger and more satisfactory job, although with too large a proportion of plates, there is just a danger of getting too much bulk in the back.

When the plates are on heavy or stiff paper, the strain on the section is relieved by breaking over the plates. This is done by taking a line a fraction wider than the distance of the tip, laying a straight-edge along it, and with the tip of the folder, bending up the edge of the plate to a sharp right angle against the straight-edge or ruler. This break must naturally be away from the tipped side so that when the plate is turned over it bends at the crease made, and does not readily lift the leaf, on which it is tipped. Some judgment is necessary when employing this method, as some plates are too brittle to allow of it. A very much better way for heavy and unyielding plates is to add a strip of strong thin paper, or better still a strip of fine jaconet to the edge of the plate, and turn it over the section in the same manner as when the plate is large enough to turn over.

In the case of exceptionally heavy plates, it is sometimes necessary to make a hinge of linen. That is to say, the plate is treated in a similar manner to the method of breaking over, only in this case, the piece is cut right off and joined up with a strip of jaconet, leaving a space slightly wider than the thickness of the plate, and the jaconet carried round the section. This method gives the maximum of strength and freedom, with the minimum of strain. In the case of plates stuck on a mount, the additional thickness is useful in balancing the extra thickness of the back. This has to be noted in making up a book. A little extra swelling in the back is helpful, too much is troublesome and unsightly, while too little is rectified by the addition of guards to the back. These guards are made of strips of paper similar to the book, about half an inch wide, folded over and placed inside the sections, throughout the book, or at the necessary places according to the make up of the individual volume.

This guarding is of utmost importance in the case of maps, diagrams, etc., that require folding, as the folded bulk must be equalized in the back.

There appears to be no general rule for the folding of

maps, for they are found in all manner of forms, and are rarely refolded in their original folds when once in use, greatly to the detriment of map and book. It is generally agreed, however, that the simplest and most serviceable method is the concertina fold. Assuming the top of the map to be flush with the head, the concertina fold is made by first bringing the bottom of the map to face itself, and making the first fold where it will escape the knife when the book is cut ; then returning the top in the opposite way, and up again if necessary ; but at each return, the position of the fold should be a fraction less, to minimize bulk as far as possible.

THE CONCERTINA FOLD

If the width of the map is also greater than the book, the same process is repeated after the tail has been folded. The distance from the back to the fold should be as great as practicable, and the distance of the edge of the upfold should be equally well clear of the back, as this is the danger point, when in use, and just where folded maps get torn if not properly relaid in their right folds.

When a map is " thrown out " it is placed on a guard the full width of the book, so that the book may be consulted at any point without the map being obscured. Sometimes the maps are only a single fold, but in that case the fold may go up to the back, attached with an added guard ; but the distance of the fold must be sufficiently clear of the back to open freely.

Generally speaking, there is sufficient guide given in the list of illustrations for the placing of plates, etc., and these should always be arranged to face the page mentioned. The frontispiece faces the title. In the case of plates that read lengthwise, the reading is placed to the right-hand side, i.e. the plates facing even numbers should have the top of the plates at the back of the book, and those facing odd numbers the top at the fore-edge. This is not an invariable rule, but it is more accepted now than it was a century ago. Failing any indication as to the placing of plates, the only thing

MAP " THROWN OUT "

possible is to read them in. This is a pleasant enough task when the subject matter of the book and the reader are in perfect harmony; but it can be a very trying occupation when the case is otherwise.

" Graingerizing " is the name given to the extra illustrating of well-known standard works, and is more the work of literary people than of the bookbinder, although the binder is often called upon to make up a book composed of a conglomeration of matter of all shapes and sizes, to say nothing of differences in paper. It is not unusual for two volumes to have had so much matter added to them as to be made into twenty or more. This almost invariably means single leaves and overcasting, larger plates being trimmed down to size, and smaller ones inlaid up to size.

In the case of such books, a very necessary precaution is to number in pencil the upper side of all plates and letterpress consecutively, at a point where it will not be trimmed off. This is a precaution against a possible misplacing in subsequent handling, and also a protection for the operator. Literary people are sometimes erratic, and not always kindly disposed towards the binder.

When a plate is inlaid to size, a piece of paper the size of the book is obtained, and of the weight, tone, and texture, of the plate as nearly as possible ; the plate is trimmed to the point from which it is determined the inlay is to commence, and is then laid on the new paper in the position required, on each corner a pinprick is made in the new leaf, and the centre cut away to the extent of one-eighth of an inch less all round. This eighth of an inch is pared to a fine edge on the upper side, and the outer edge of the plate is correspondingly pared on the under side, the plate is next laid face downwards, and the piece cut away from the new leaf, is placed on the plate so as to expose the pared eighth evenly all round. This exposed edge is well pasted, the paper removed, and the plate placed to the pin-holes, well rubbed down, and left to dry under a light pressure. The larger plates are trimmed to size with properly balanced margins. This may be done with a thick piece of glass with a perfectly smooth edge such as is used by photographers. If a glass is obtainable the right size, this can be placed over the page until it gives a perfectly balanced margin, and then the four edges trimmed to size. With miscellaneous work, however, it is not always practicable to obtain glass the size of each book, and so a larger one may be taken, and a dark piece of paper pasted to two of the edges, leaving exposed glass to the size of the page. The plate is then placed on the glass in such a way as to get perfect balance, and the two edges trimmed. The plate is then turned round and the two trimmed edges laid flush with the dark paper, thus exposing the remaining two edges, which can be trimmed in their turn.

There is no fixed rule by which margins may be determined, one's aesthetic sense being generally the best guide. Usually the balance is found with equal margins on the sides, but substantially more margin at the tail than head, varying according to the balance or framing of the picture itself.

## CHAPTER V

### DRY-CLEANING, WASHING, AND MENDING

DRY-CLEANING is frequently necessary with old books, but it must be done with extreme care. The paper is often so tender and perished that irreparable damage can be done very easily.

Breadcrumbs are useful, or a very soft rubber if the paper will stand it. Marks may often be removed by rubbing in a circular direction with a piece of paper the same texture as the leaf to be cleaned. In very good paper, cuttle fish bone may be used for very bad marks ; and in extreme cases, very fine glass-paper (the sharpness taken off by rubbing two pieces together) may be used on the margins. The rubbing movement must always be toward the edges to avoid tearing.

Dry-cleaning will, of course, remove only surface dirt. Stains in the paper will mean washing. Whatever the stains may be, if there be surface dirt on the leaf, it must be dry-cleaned first, as any washing or sizing will fix in surface dirt, and make it almost, if not quite, impossible to remove afterwards.

Fox-marks are the stains most commonly met with in old books, and one must admit, regretfully, on some modern ones, especially good hand-made paper editions. What these stains are exactly, or how they are caused, is a matter on which experts do not seem to agree. The two outstanding opinions are : on the one hand, that they are caused by colloids of iron getting into the paper during some process of its manufacture ; and on the other, that it is a fungus growth arising from the size in the paper. Whatever the cause, it is known to yield to the following treatment: the marked sheets are first put into a bath of very hot water in which a little permanganate of potash has been diluted, and left in that bath from five to fifteen minutes, according to the density of the stain and the strength of the chemical. It is then removed to another bath of hot water to which a little sulphurous acid has been added, and left in this until the bleaching process has been completed.

It is almost impossible to give quantities with any certainty, as the density of the stains and the nature of the paper vary so enormously; experience is the safest guide. If the acid does not remove the stain entirely, it may be necessary for the sheet to go back into a stronger solution of permanganate and remain there a little longer before being bleached again. The leaf is next removed into a bath of clean hot water, to clear away any effects of the chemicals. It is then blotted off and allowed to dry, to be ready for sizing and toning.

A more ready method is to pass the sheet through a bath of hot water, to which has been added a little chloride of lime in solution. This is a very drastic method, which should be resorted to only in extreme cases; but, if precautions are taken thoroughly to wash out the lime afterwards, no harm will be done to the fibre of the paper. Ordinary writing ink can be removed by the addition of oxalic acid to the lime bath.

The process of washing will have removed a large amount of the original size from the paper, so the paper has to be resized and toned back to its original colour. Good quality clean skin glue makes a suitable size when passed through a fine sieve. The quantity required varies with the absorbent quality of the paper and the hardness desired. It is not wise to get the paper too brittle; but it is good to get old paper nice and firm.

The necessary colouring, to restore the tone to the

paper, is put in with the size. Burnt sugar, coffee, chicory, and stout are among the colourings used, but practically any colouring matter may be utilized to obtain the desired effect.

The size bath is just warm and the sheets are left in sufficiently long to enable the size to work itself well into the paper. Double leaves may then be blotted off, and hung up to dry on a line when practicable, while single leaves may be laid flat on a hard paper and occasionally turned over whilst drying. A whole book may be put into a bath, in double leaves, opened out, and removed in double leaves, but nipped in a laying press in bulk. The surplus size is squeezed out while the book is in a vertical position, a receptacle being placed under the press to receive the waste size. Each double leaf is then separated and hung up to dry.

The cleaning of old books is a practice requiring a vast amount of care, experience, and initiative ; and this experience should have been gained on books of little value before the handling of valuable old books is attempted.

Sometimes old paper is so fragile in the bath, that it is impossible to lift the sheet out with the fingers. A thin board or good stout paper under the sheet will, however, enable it to be removed with safety, as the old paper will cling to the new, thus avoiding the likelihood of tearing.

Old papers, and some modern ones, can be mended in such a way as to defy detection. The first and most important matter is to find a piece of paper exactly matching the book to be mended. For invisible mending this is often the most costly part of the process, and the most essential. The two pieces of paper (viz. the one to be mended and the one to be used for mending) are both unsized by being passed through a bath of hot water ; then, when dry, the piece to be joined on is shaped to complete the missing part, but allowed to overlap an eighth of an inch. The two parts that come together are pared away with a small and very sharp knife leaving a ragged edge to each, and then the two pared edges are joined together. The paste used in mending is made from equal parts of cornflour and wheaten-flour, to the consistency of a not too thick cream.

Great care is taken, in joining, to see that the wire lines in the papers are made to match ; and the fibres on the edges of the join kept loose. When the papers are thoroughly dry, a little judicious scraping will remedy any undue bulk at the splice. The mended sheet has next to be resized and great care is here necessary to avoid the separation of the two pieces. It is a good precaution to pass the sheet through the size bath within a folded piece of blotting paper. The size will pass through the blotting paper, which will in its turn keep the mended leaf together. It can then be blotted off on a fresh piece, and eventually be allowed to dry flat as in ordinary sizing. An alternative method is to size each side of the sheet with a very wide soft brush, allowing each side to dry separately.

The results that have been achieved in this direction during the last century by a very few individuals in France and England, are amazing in their perfection, and even where parts of the text are lacking, a facsimile of the missing portion can be made so skilfully as to defy detection.

A fairly neat mend can be made by splicing in the same manner as described, but without unsizing the paper and consequently with no resizing. Tears may be joined by pasting both edges of the tear and joining them up, so that the projecting fibres of each link up, and then laying along each side a piece of fine Japanese paper, the whole being well rubbed down and left to dry; when it is dry, the surplus tissue is scraped away, and it will be found that the strong loose fibres of the Japanese tissue have clung to the mended part, and, after their removal, the join will, if done with skill and judgment, be strong, neat, and almost invisible.

It is sometimes necessary to split a sheet of paper, as for instance, when a good portrait that has been printed on the other side may be disfigured by the print showing through. This splitting may be done by well pasting on both sides the paper to be split, with good flour paste, preferably on a sheet of glass, so that the paste is not removed when the second side is pasted. It is then laid between two pieces of jaconet, or between two pieces of good smooth handmade paper, and well pressed to ensure that every particle of both surfaces shall stick to the paper or jaconet. It is then allowed to dry to the point when both surfaces have well adhered to the jaconet; but with sufficient moisture inside the paper to allow the fibres of the softened paper to yield. The two pieces of jaconet are then pulled apart, when half the leaf will be found clinging to one piece, and the corresponding half to the other. Both portions are then put separately in a bath of warm water with the jaconet underneath, when, after a while, they will separate, and each split leaf can be removed by using a strong piece of paper to which it is allowed to cling, after which it can be blotted off and left to dry.

A newspaper portrait split in this manner, and mounted on a hand-made paper, with a plate mark, is fit to illustrate quite a good book. A rather severe test was once given when a binder was called upon to split a leaf of one of the Oxford India paper Prayer Books. The Confirmation Service finished at the bottom of one page, and the Marriage Service began at the top of the other. The book was required for a wedding, and an illuminated page giving a record of the wedding was immediately to precede the wedding service. When the two split leaves were remounted, it was impossible to see that they had been interfered with. It would be unwise, however, for the novice to practise on India paper.

For books with folded maps or plans required for hard wear, it is frequently necessary to mount these on linen. A moderately soft fabric with a smooth surface, and of a substance suited to the size of the book is selected. A table with a smooth unvarnished surface without any joints or pronounced grain of wood showing is used for laying down the linen. A very good surface can be obtained from a selected sheet of three-ply wood, with a well-sanded surface lightly dusted with French chalk. The fabric is cut 2 in. or 3 in. larger all round than the size of the map to be mounted, and pinned down on the board all round the edges at a distance of 2 in. or 3 in., and stretched as tightly as possible without the slightest sign of a crease or wrinkle. The map is then well pasted, and the paste allowed to sink in for about five minutes, when, in the case of very thick paper, a second application of paste may be necessary.

The map is next laid perfectly even on the linen, and well rubbed down ; first with the flat of the hands, and then with a folder over a good strong paper. All air bubbles are removed, and the rubbing action is always from the middle toward the edges, when, if the paper should stretch causing a crease, the map is lifted up to that point, and laid down again against the pressure of the hand. The adhesion at the edges requires special attention. When all is thoroughly stuck down and lying perfectly flat, a period of twelve hours is allowed for drying. The pins are then removed, and, if there is a slight clinging of the linen to the board when lifted, it is a sure indication that the paste has penetrated the material, which can only be separated in water.

The projecting linen is next trimmed off, the map folded as required, and laid under a very heavy pressure overnight.

It is sometimes useful to leave a piece of projecting linen untrimmed at a point where the map is joined to the book. This acts as a very secure and useful guard, and, if a piece of paper is stuck on to this portion, it can be folded to equal the thickness of the map, thus forming a complete section in itself. It is sometimes found, especially in maps of thick brittle paper requiring several folds, that the constant folding injures the surface of the paper at the folds; this may be avoided by cutting the folds before mounting and laying the pieces of the map on the linen so as to leave a slight space between the two pieces, making the bend in the linen and not in the map. The space is determined according to the fold. If the map is folded concertina-wise, and from the tail first, the horizontal spaces are only a fraction wider than double the thickness of the paper; the vertical spaces are determined by the number of folds from the tail, enabling them to bend over without strain. For instance: Three folds up will mean a space of six papers and linens.

*By courtesy of Messrs. John Greig & Sons*

THE NIPPING MACHINE

When the good stout old hand-made paper was of necessity in general use and the pressure of the printing press greater than it is to-day, the printed part of the sheet was thinner than the margins, and caused corrugations across the middle of the pages. It was the binder's work to remove these, which he did by using a gold-beater's hammer on the margins and so equalizing the thickness. There are not many binders to-day who would have the courage to use a beating hammer, especially on valuable old books, as that method is fraught with such grave danger to the book from an unpractised hand.

One English firm, with a long and honourable record behind it, suffered a serious strike through dropping the beating hammer, and introducing the rolling machine, which was an innovation at the time. It is quite probable that, if the process were reversed to-day, and the beating hammer restored, another strike would follow the imposition of such terrible manual work.

The rolling machine is very similar to the familiar domestic mangle, only much stronger, and having steel rollers. The book is passed through it a few sections at a time, giving a good solid book as the result.

The days of the rolling machine are numbered, however, as the engineer has reverted to the principle of the beating hammer, and produced a machine called a "nipping" machine, which brings together two flat surfaces from a revolving eccentric, giving a powerful beating movement that will give a fairly solid book in a very few moments.

# CHAPTER VI

## SEWING

If we assume that due consideration has been given to the sound practical foundation of folded sections in the books to be bound, the next thing to be considered is the binding of these sections securely together, yet allowing each leaf to open freely. What exactly was the earliest method of joining sections together can only be a matter for conjecture; but it is fairly safe to assume that each of these sections was originally stitched down the middle, and the loose ends tied together, which would be a fairly obvious way of handling a number of insetted sections, and the principle is not far removed from our present-day methods, even if the latest developments in machine sewing be taken into consideration.

It is still the custom in firms which boast of soundness and durability of work, to follow the methods adopted by the monks of the Middle Ages, who were practically the only followers of the craft in their day. Even the frames on which they worked have not been altered in the slightest degree.

This early method of sewing the sections together is known as " flexible " sewing. Exactly when that name was given to it is difficult to say; but it is safe to assume that its original name was something very different, for anything less flexible than those old monastic bindings can hardly be conceived. That fact, however, was more the result of subsequent treatment than any fault in the principle of the sewing.

The frame on which this hand-sewing is done consists

of a flat bed of wood, large enough to take a full size folio, raised from the table with batons of wood at each end. Along the front edge of this bed a slot is cut out about half an inch wide running the whole length between the batons. Fixed at each end almost in a line with the slot, are two uprights about 2 ft. high, with a screw thread running almost the whole length. Across these uprights runs a bar of wood with holes at each end to correspond with the position and circumference of these pillars. On each upright, a wooden screw nut is placed for the cross-bar to rest on; they also serve to move it to any desired position. The position of the cross-bar is so arranged that a perpendicular line drawn from the inner edge of the slot in the base would go through the middle of the cross-bar. On this cross-bar are affixed a number of cords, known as "lay bands." The usual number is five, according to the number of cords on which the book is to be sewn. The lay bands are separate loops, the ends securely knotted together, giving a circumference about three times that of the cross-bar.

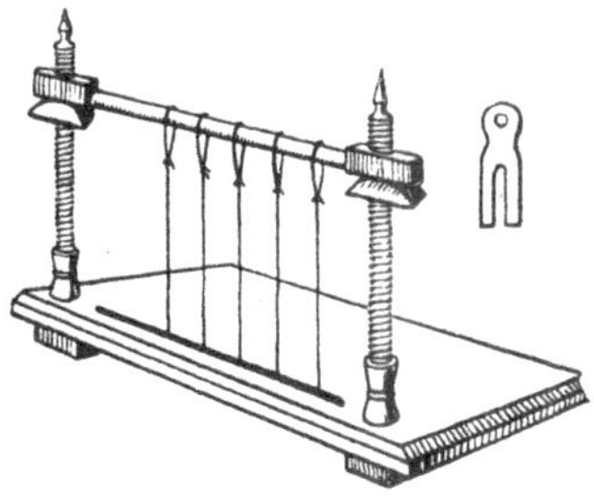

HAND-SEWING FRAME

The cords, or "bands" as they are called, to which the sections are to be sewn, are attached first to the lay bands with a slipknot, then on to what are known as "keys," which go through and across the slot at the base. The keys are pieces of metal about an eighth of an inch in thickness, $1\frac{1}{2}$ in. long, and $\frac{1}{2}$ in. in width, shaped not unlike a tuning fork, but with a neck and head at one end.

To attach the cord to the key, the forked end of the key is laid flat under the front of the base of the sewing frame, the cord brought straight down tightly under the right-hand side of the neck, held in position underneath with the fingers of the left hand whilst the key is removed, the cord is next twisted round the neck of the key, then the fork end of the key is turned over on the cord holding it in position ; the key is then passed through the slot at the base and fixed across with the sewing cord resting against the back of the slot perpendicularly. When all the cords have been set up in the same way and the spaces properly adjusted, the nuts are screwed up to raise the cross-bar and so tighten the bands. It requires some training to fix the tension of the cords evenly so that they can all be screwed up equally tight, which is very essential.

The selection of the cords is also very important. There should be very little dressing in them, and the strands of which they are made must be exceptionally long. The thickness and strength are determined by the size, weight and thickness of the book, and the nature of the paper. A small India paper Prayer Book requires cord very little thicker than a stout thread, while a folio book on heavy paper requires a cord fully an eighth of an inch thick, if not more.

For the average book the accepted custom is to sew on five bands, evenly spaced between the cords, one-third larger space at the tail, and an eighth larger at the head. It is advisable to mark the position of the cords on the book, then to set the bands to the marking. In addition to the bands, the kettle-stitches are marked also, and these are generally sawn in sufficiently deep to bury the knots made in the sewing. The kettle-stitch at the tail is conveniently made at a position equidistant from the bottom band, as the band is above it, and the one at the head is made about a quarter of the distance down from the head to the first panel. The name kettle-stitch is probably a corruption of the words catch-up stitch, as the threads enter and leave the sections at these points, and are then made to link, or catch up one another.

The use of good unbleached linen thread is always advisable and it should be of a substance suited to the weight of the section. As a general guide, number thirty, three cord, is suitable for the average crown octavo book, and the range may run from fifty, two cord, to twelve, three cord. Long needles (preferably egg-eyed straws, number 1, 2, or 3, according to the thickness of the thread) and as long a length of thread taken each time as can be conveniently worked so as to avoid too many joins.

The operator sits sideways with the left arm between the last cord and the upright of the frame, or " press " as it is more generally called. The section is picked up with the left hand and opened in the centre, beginning with the first one and laying it in its exact position opposite the cords, as previously marked on the back. The needle enters the kettle-stitch, travels along the inside of the section, and comes out behind the first cord ; the thread being pulled along until only about an inch or so is left sticking out of the kettle-stitch. The thread is carried round the cord, and through the same hole in the section, out again behind the second cord, and then drawn quite tightly. This is repeated at all the cords until the thread comes out eventually at the other kettle-stitch. Thus, the section has a thread running through it from one kettle-stitch to the other, and firmly knotted to five cords. The point at which the thread enters and leaves the section should be the tangential junction of the section and the cord.

Care must be taken on re-entering the section that the thread is not pierced with the needle. Each time the thread leaves the section it must be pulled tight round the preceding band, and the direction of the pull must be the way the thread is travelling. The next section is treated in a similar manner, with the thread travelling in the opposite direction, and then knotted to the end left out of the first kettle-stitch. The third section is

SEWING BY HAND

treated as the first, and then the thread leaving the last kettle-stitch is looped round the connecting portion between the first and second section, and then again between the second and third before starting on the fourth section. This looping up with the two preceding sections is carried right through the book to the end; the final result being that a continuous thread runs through the whole of the book, carried round a cord at five points and each section doubly knotted together at both ends.

When one length of thread runs out, a new piece is

joined to it by what is known as a weaver's knot, which is the smallest possible knot, and this is always arranged to fall inside the section between two cords. The threads give a swelling to the back of the book which is of great value in subsequent processes; but one danger always to be avoided is the pulling of the knots in the kettle-stitches too tightly, thereby reducing the necessary swelling at these points.

This method of sewing can be justly claimed to possess the soundest principles of construction. It was adopted by the monks, with some variations, for the binding of their beautifully illuminated missals on vellum. The variations were, chiefly, the use of leather or vellum thongs in place of cords; the thongs being frequently double the ordinary width required, but cut open down the middle to the depth of the thickness of the book. In this case the thread came out through the cut in the thong, right round the two divisions, and in again at the same hole. Double cords were sometimes used, the thread being carried round in the same way. The double cords, and divided thongs, have an advantage in principle over the single ones, as the section is better supported against the pull of the thread, where most required, at the point of leaving and re-entering it.

For dictionaries, devotional books, and the like, that have hard wear and must open very freely, the double cords have the additional advantage of giving good support to the back, without undue thickness of cord. For very free opening, the minimum of thickness of cord must be aimed at, consistent with the necessary support and strength proportionate to the book.

Another method of sewing, known as "tape sewing," is adopted almost universally for stationery work; very frequently for lending-library work, and occasionally for general work. The thread does not go round the tape as in flexible sewing, but merely behind it. For very heavy ledgers and the like, when good strong webbing can be used, the maximum of support is given to the back with the minimum of resistance against the free opening.

Ordinary or "sawn in" sewing is the method that has been most widely adopted for general miscellaneous letterpress work, for well over a century. It merely means that recesses are made in the back of the book with a saw, sufficiently deep to bury the cords flush with the back, and the thread goes behind the cord, as in tape sewing, and not round as in the case of flexible sewing.

Much controversy has ranged round this method of sewing for more than a generation, and there is no intention of taking sides in the matter here; but it may be pointed out, whilst the mutilation of the back is open to just protest, the test of time has shown that, in the course of years, the perishing of the covering leather, and the accompanying perishing of the exposed threads and cords, of the flexible book, tend to its more ready collapse than is the case with the much despised and so-called mutilated sawn-in book of the same period, with its protected thread and cord. The examples of flexibly sewn work, many centuries old, that remain with us quite sound, have still some acid-free leather, and glue protecting the cords and threads. The covering glue has been baked so hard, that it is impossible to open the books into the back: that fact mainly accounting for their preservation through the ages.

The form of sewing of a temporary character, generally adopted by the French publishers for their paper-covered publications, is known in this country as "French" sewing. The thread enters the section at the kettle-stitch, travels along the section, and comes out about one-third of the distance along; it then goes up into the second section to a distance of about the second third, and then re-enters the first section at the same point, continuing the remaining third to the kettle-stitch. This principle of holding together two sections on one thread is carried out throughout the book, the knot in the kettle-stitch being the main support for holding the sections together, and possesses the advantage of being readily pulled to pieces again, for permanent binding, without injury to the sections. The exit and return to the section may be made at more points if desirable. This method of holding together two sections with one thread is sometimes adopted in sawn-in work, as it reduces the swelling in thick books with numerous thin sections. For permanent work it is not sound, and should only be adopted in extreme cases.

The development of machinery for sewing books has been very extensive in recent years. The main lines on which their inventors have worked, being on the principle of tape sewing, with, perhaps, one great advantage over the hand-sewing method, in so far, that the stitching is interlocked. The speed at which these machines can be worked is about as fast as the operator can pick up the sections and feed them on the machine.

One of the most recent machines despises the idea of sections and thread altogether, and takes the book as a whole, in single leaves, gives a free application of glue, and relies on that alone for holding the leaves together. The idea was used nearly a century ago when certain types of books were bound up in single leaves by the application of caoutchouc on the back, supported with a covering of strong linen. It was remarkable how flexible and strong these books were, until the rubber began to perish, and to-day a large majority of the books so treated are simply collections of loose leaves.

In the more modern developments of this idea it is all a question of cost, and it s not improbable that the binding will last as long as the book. Whatever may be said against this popular series of books, their designer has at least been consistent, for the principle of binding is just about as sound as the paper.

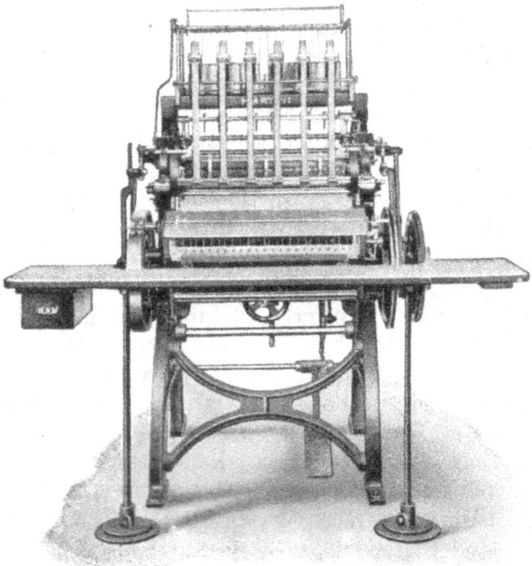

*By courtesy of* *Messrs. Friedheim*

FRIEDHEIM'S SIMPLIFIED BOOK SEWING MACHINE CAPABLE OF SEWING 60 SECTIONS PER MINUTE AND 4 TAPES ON A 6-INCH BOOK

This question of the soundness, or lack of it, of much of our modern paper has been engaging the attention of public, and other librarians, for some time past ; for they found that, however well the books may have been bound they would still persist in falling away from their bindings, leaving both covers and foundations intact.

To obviate this, instead of the sewing lying in the folds at the back, these folds were cut away, the books divided into convenient sections, and overcast in the manner described previously ; but with the important difference that the second section was overcast through

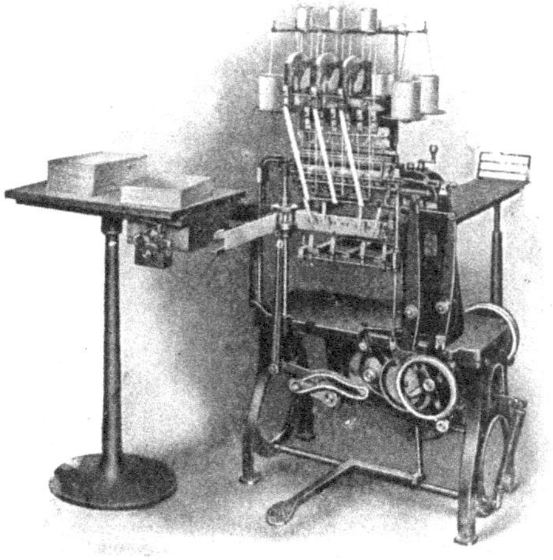

*By courtesy of* *Messrs. Smyth-Horne, Ltd.*

SMYTH BOOK SEWING MACHINE, CAPABLE OF SEWING 60 SECTIONS PER MINUTE

into the first, the third into the second, and so on through the book, giving a solidly overcast book, gripped to the extent of over an eighth of an inch with the thread and with judicious glueing up afterwards, the glue being allowed to run into the back as far as the depth of the stitches if possible. This method, although repugnant to many binders, has proved to be more durable for inferior paper than the orthodox methods.

America has quite recently produced an over-sewing machine on this principle, and the exhaustive tests made on lending library work have proved its great value. The speed at which the machine can be fed is truly

*By courtesy of* *The T. W. & C. B. Sheridan Co., Ltd.*

OVERSEWING MACHINE

This machine performs the type of book sewing that is variously known as "overcasting," "whip-stitching," "library sewing," and "oversewing," and is capable of doing nearly ten times as much as sewing by hand.

remarkable, and in spite of what appears to the contrary, books properly treated in the subsequent processes open very freely. Indeed, so successful has this method proved that many librarians stipulate it in their specifications.

# CHAPTER VII

## END PAPERS

THE end papers of a book serve both a decorative and a utilitarian purpose. They act as a protection for each end of the book, and also as a lining to the board after covering. The ancients, with their oak boards, sometimes ignored their use altogether; but, to speak generally, end papers have been considered a necessary part of the binder's work from the earliest times. They have been, and still are for that matter, very varied in character; and their attachment has been tried in many different ways. When nothing but vellum, and good hand-made paper, were used in the making up of books, they often served their purpose by the addition of a folded sheet of vellum or paper similar to the rest of the book, consisting of two leaves stitched at the beginning and the end, as in an ordinary section—the one leaf to paste down on the inside of the board, and the other as a protection for the book. It was only the fine quality and strength of the material that made such a method practicable.

When two folded leaves were used, one insetted into the other and sewn on as before, stronger results were obtained. The first leaf was used as a protection during the processes of binding, being eventually torn away, except for about 1 in. strip at the back which was left on for added strength at the joint. The strip of the first, and the whole of the second leaf, were finally pasted together over the board, leaving two protecting leaves at either end of the book.

For more than a century the most generally accepted

papers for book ends in permanent bindings have been "marble" papers of an infinite variety of patterns. These papers were first introduced into this country by the Dutch, but their origin is probably Persian. Some of them have the colours arranged in such a way as to resemble marble: hence the name.

There are many secrets and tricks in connection with the making of these papers, and at present the whole art is in the hands of a very few individuals; and some of these do not possess all the secrets known to their forerunners in the art. The main principle is the throwing, by means of splashes from a brush, of a variety of colours on the surface of a trough of size or gum, and by mixing more or less ox-gall in the colours to make them spread, so forming veins and blobs as required. Some varieties have combs of varying widths drawn through the size, either straight or zigzag, with a resulting variety of effect. The paper is laid flat on this surface, and the colour adheres to it, when it is carefully lifted off again, dried, and sometimes burnished afterwards.

A favourite style of paper at one period was a paper with a surface body of even colour on it, and again, for quite a large number of years, papers with printed patterns were largely used. In more recent years plain coloured or toned papers have been in favour, but the marble paper seems still to get back into favour for good bindings, although there are many jazz patterns on the less permanent type of book. The majority of these papers are so disfigured on the back that they require to be made up, to cover this disfigurement. These are technically known as "made ends." One folded white is pasted on one of its exterior sides, the folded marble is laid evenly on this with the folds of both papers together, and on the underneath side of the white is tipped a protection sheet. This is brought over the two folds and so protects the portion of the end paper which is to be pasted down from injury in subsequent processes. These papers are then nipped just for a few minutes, while the moisture is in them, and then hung up to dry, then nipped again, when they will dry perfectly flat. This end paper consists of one protection sheet (an odd leaf of any good paper will answer this purpose), one leaf of marble paper which will eventually be pasted down on the inside of the board, one leaf of marble and white stuck together, and one leaf of single white. The final effect then is that, on opening the board, a balance of the opposing pages is presented again, with the two following pages of white the same balance is obtained, then the final page of the end and the half-title are brought into harmony. As far as is practicable, the white should be similar in tone and character to the rest of the book. Insetted white ends are made by taking two folded whites, and insetting one into the other by tipping the inset on to the side of the leaf next to the book. The result then is, the first white becomes the protection sheet, the second white the paste down, the third and fourth being fly-leaves. This method is frequently done with coloured body paper, the inset being the coloured paper. On small books this is sometimes necessary, as the two pasted papers may be too heavy for the size of the book.

The attachment of these ends to the book presents some problems. It is quite obvious that, in made end-papers, to sew through the white is not practicable, especially when it would be called upon to hold five leaves. In the case of the insetted white, while there are two folds to sew through, the threads would show in the joint of the book, and this is generally considered unsightly, and certainly is not very strong at a point where strength is most necessary. The alternative then would appear to be, to tip them on the first and last leaves of the book; but to expect four or five leaves to hang on to one single leaf is asking too much of the average modern paper.

If the first and last sections have been previously overcast, then the tipping has a fair chance to hold, for it is tipped to a solid section, and, that section being tipped to the next one is made still more solid, and this tipping both sides hides the otherwise unsightly over-casting. The very presence of this over-casting is sometimes objected to, and with some measure of justification in the case of flexible books, for it prevents these first and last few leaves from opening right up to the back.

Recent years have seen a revival of a form of end paper which claims to overcome all difficulties without any of the objections mentioned. Two folded whites are tipped together at the folded end, facing opposite directions and overlapping about a quarter of an inch. It being assumed that these two tipped leaves are lying parallel with the operator, with the overlaid part of the fold facing away, the first leaf is pulled toward the operator until it is even with the overlaid fold, the whole of the end is turned over, and the remaining leaf folded over on itself, flush with the previous fold, and inside this last fold is insetted a folded white. This is called the zigzag end paper, and a glance at it endways will give the obvious origin of its name. It is attached by sewing as a single section, the thread going through the insetted white. The first leaf is the protection leaf, the second the paste-down, and four flys follow, the first of these flys being attached on the return part of the zigzag of the last fly. The advantage of this end paper is, that it has a double fold to sew through without any threads appearing in the fold of the joint. It has the added advantage of forming an open V shape in the joint, which yields to the opening of the boards, and takes off any possible strain in the opening. The main objection raised to this end paper is the excessive number of flys preceding the book, yet to some minds this fact constitutes a great advantage.

If a marble, or other paper requiring one side to be pasted over, is desired in this form of end, it can quite readily be made. One folded white is pasted all over one of its outer sides, and the other one is tipped to the extent of a quarter of an inch, and overlaid on the first in the same manner as before, with the pasted side up: the folded marble paper is then laid on across the two white papers, the fold being laid flush with the edge of the tip, and the tip being flush with the fold of the white. An elongated V shape is formed between the marble and the white, and the one is folded back over the marble, and the other over the white. The result is, one protection leaf, one marble paste-down, one pasted marble and white together, and two white flys. The merits and demerits of this end paper may well be left to individual judgment.

As a contrast to the elaborate methods of making ends already described, and still practised by many binders, the very great majority of machine-produced books have a single folded white tipped on to the first and last leaves and left at that. For very heavy books it is sometimes advisable to fix a strip of cloth in the joint for added strength. One of the most popular methods is to overcast together the first section to the ends, whatever they are, but *minus* the board paper, and *plus* the strip of cloth facing towards the book. The line of overcasting is most important in this case, as it must correspond with the base of the joint when the book is backed. In pasting down, the cloth returns on itself from the base of the joint, and on to the boards ; the board paper being added separately. The only objection to this method is the usual one of overcasting ; but its strength and neatness are unquestionable.

For stationery books and books with a French joint, the cloth is usually attached between the marble and white and sewn as a section, this being quite a suitable method for tape-sewn books.

There are other forms of ends in use, but in the main they are individual modifications of one or more of those already described, and each has its own claim according to the uses to which it is put.

# CHAPTER VIII

## FORWARDING

THE sewing of a book constitutes the foundation of the future work, and it is much to be regretted that many fine bindings do not have the foundations that their covers naturally lead one to expect.

Some of the early binders did not cover their books, but only attached to the cords on which they were sewn a pair of good, sound, wooden boards, and left it at that. These books were sewn on leather thongs. The boards are a quarter of an inch or more in thickness, with a long slanting bevel both sides of the board towards the back, to take up the swelling in the back on the inside, and the thickness of the laced-in cords on the outside. They are made flush with the back but project beyond the other three edges, and the insides of these edges have a sharp bevel extending from the contact with the book outwards. Holes are pierced opposite the cords about half an inch in, and more holes a further half an inch in. Recesses are made to take the thongs, which are laced through the top side, and out again from the inside, and the last hole plugged with a wooden pin, the ends of the thong and plug being cut flush.

It must soon have become obvious to the old binders that the swelling in the back caused by the position of the threads directly over one another required some consideration; for, while they could maintain a perfectly flat back during the process of binding, the frequent opening would soon make an objectionable concave. This natural swelling was soon turned to good account and the book was made convex, still having sufficient swelling to make a joint to take the boards; and to-day the process of rounding, backing, lacing-in the boards, and cutting the edges, is called "forwarding."

Assume the book to be sewn, the end papers attached and the cords left projecting about $1\frac{1}{2}$ in. beyond the back each side: the ends of cord are first untwisted and each separate strand opened out with a bodkin, until the whole of the cords right from the edge of the back are simply a series of straight fibres. The back and the head are knocked up flat and square between a pair of protecting boards; the cords, or as they are now called the "slips," being under the protecting boards. The back is then covered with a coating of thin glue to fill in the spaces between the sections, and incidentally to hold the back together for the subsequent rounding. The rounding is done when the glue is in a state of flexibility. It should be sufficiently moist to enable the book to be moulded into the round, and yet not tacky enough to stick to the hammer. The book is laid flat on the table with the back away from the operator, the left hand being laid on the sides, and the thumb on the fore-edge. The upper portion is pulled over until the back faces up at rather a sharp angle, the back is then gently tapped with the hammer on the upper portion, and the sections readily yield to this pressure. The book is then turned over and treated similarly on the other side. Several turns of the book are sometimes necessary before the right shape is formed. The thumb in the fore-edge is a big factor in moulding the shape of the back. Individual taste must determine this shape. Some prefer the shape to be almost semicircular, others semi-elliptical, while many favour an almost flat or semi-flat back. These shapes may generally be determined at will if the swelling has been controlled previously. A book with a big swelling in the back will naturally fall into a big round, and one with too little swelling will be difficult to get into a good round. Thick thread and free sewing will give a good swelling to the back ; thin thread, and tightly hammered down sections during the sewing process, may reduce the swelling to almost nothing. The shape of the back should be considered in the early stages of the work so as to minimize the difficulties later.

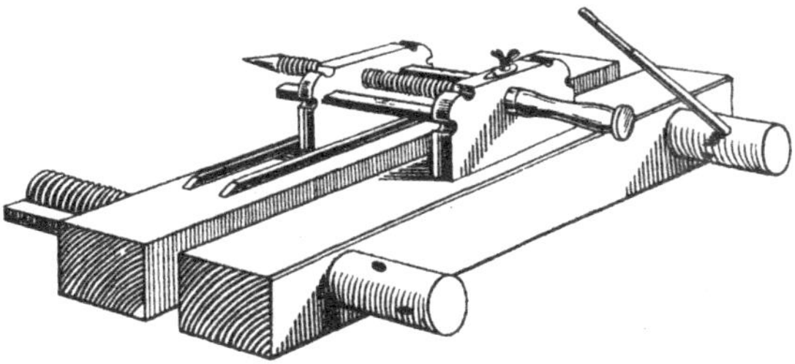

LAYING PRESS

The whole of the swelling should not be taken up in the round, for it is necessary to reserve some of it for the joints which equalize the thickness of the boards. The making of the joints is called " backing " ; for this purpose a laying press and a pair of backing boards are used. The laying press consists of two pieces of wood about 3 ft. in length, and 6 in. square, with a large wooden screw at each end to open and close the two cheeks. In one cheek the screws run free, and in the other they run in threads. There are holes in the free sides of the screws in which an iron pin is placed for leverage. The backing boards consist of a pair of wedge-shaped boards nearly as wide as the book, and a little longer, from ½ in. to 1 in. in thickness at the thickest end, and tapering from the long side at an angle of 45 degrees.

These backing boards are laid each side of the book, parallel with the joint, at a distance of the thickness of the board to be subsequently attached, *plus* the amount taken up in the bend-over of the joint, say, about a quarter more than its thickness. The tapering portion of the backing boards runs away from the book, the longest side resting against it. The boards are kept perfectly square, held firmly in the left hand, and lowered into the press until the thickest part of the boards is level with the top of the cheeks of the press. The press is then tightly and evenly screwed up first with the hands, and then with the pin, the wedge-shaped backing boards making it easy to get the book into position.

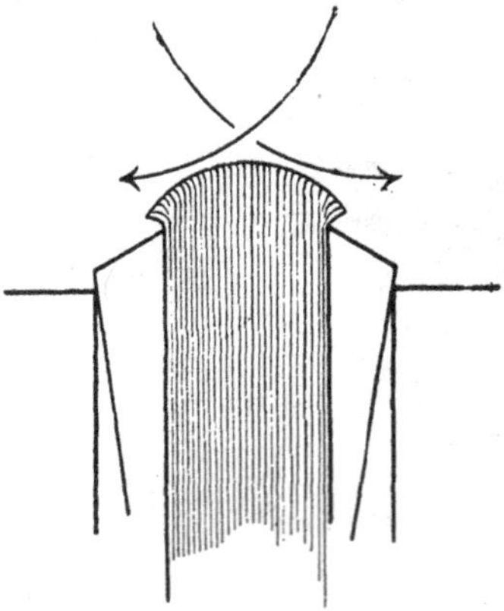

BACKING BOARDS AND BOOK

This pressure will have emphasized the swelling in the back, and it remains only to make use of the swelling, by hammering down each side of the back until a projection has been made which will take the thickness of the boards, and remains at right angles with the side of the book.

The theory of the perfectly backed book is: that the middle sections are untouched, but the sections begin to bend away from the middle in perfect gradation, until the first and last sections bend at a sharply accentuated and permanently creased right angle, maintaining a good even slope from the crown of the back to both extremes, with a good round shoulder to support the boards.

The hammer used is similar to the cobbler's hammer, the long, flat side being used to bring over the sections roughly to be finished off with the other side, which is smooth and round. The movements of the hammer are always circular, and in a direction away from the centre. By some craftsmen the methods of rounding and backing described will be considered quite obsolete, but it is still the practice of many of the best binders to retain these methods, as they claim to get the best results with them. They are also the foundation on which the more commercial methods of the present generation were based. One of the first diversions from this practice was the rounding machine, which pushes over the sections in the same way as the hammer knocks them over, and which may be said to be little more than a very long hammer with mechanical power behind it. In conjunction with this, there is the "Star" backing machine which grips the book between iron jaws, while a large roller is brought over the middle of the book, working backwards and forwards on an adjustable pivot, and so giving the back any desired shape. This method is also pressure as against hammering, but the principle remains the same.

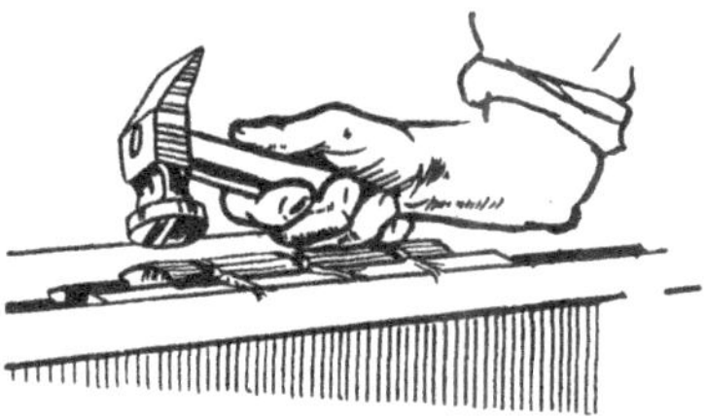

BACKING IN LAYING PRESS

By most progressive firms, these two machines have long since been relegated to the scrap heap as being too slow and cumbersome for long runs. Machines now do both processes together. The back is placed to a gauge, automatically gripped, and, with concave surfaces working in conjunction with the grip, the back is forced round and backed at the same time. These two operations are performed as fast as the books can be fed into the machine.

*By courtesy of* *Messrs. Krause*

ROUNDING MACHINE

Following the time-honoured method of in-board work, the boards are attached after the rounding and backing. The term, "in-board forwarding," is understood to mean that the boards are laced on to the cords on which the book has been sewn, and then the book is cut in the boards. "Out-board work" is understood to mean that the book is first cut, and the boards attached to the book afterwards. Both are distinct from "case" books, which do not have the boards laced in at all.

For in-board work, the boards are cut square to size, leaving a square beyond the three edges of the book,

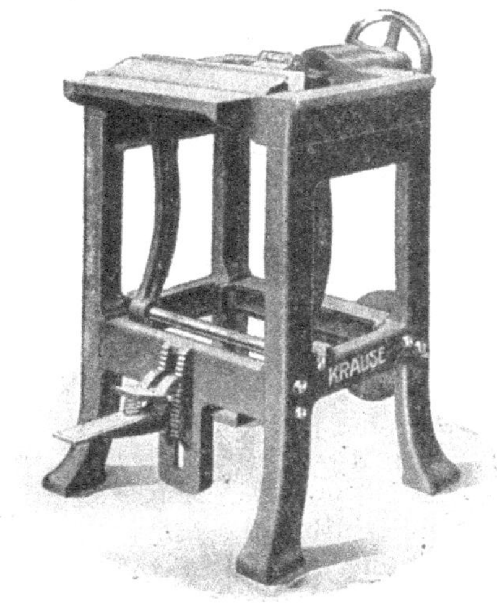

By courtesy of Messrs. Krause

HAND-BACKING MACHINE FOR USE WITH HAMMER

STAR HAND-BACKING MACHINE SHOWING USE OF ROLLER

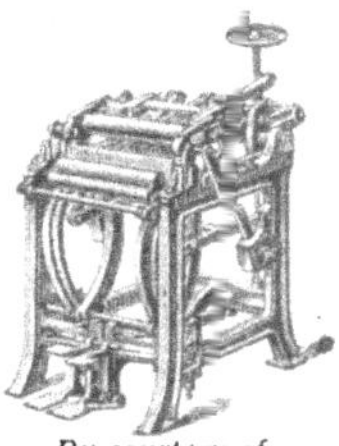

HAND-BACKING MACHINE WITH ROLLER

By courtesy of Messrs. Krause

when finally cut. The "square" of a binding is that portion which projects beyond the edges, and the size of the squares is entirely a matter of individual taste. After cutting, the boards are laid in the position on the book in which they will finally rest, and a mark is made with a pencil opposite each of the cords. The boards are then removed on to a piece of either wood or lead, and with bodkin and hammer, holes are made through them exactly opposite the cords, and about a quarter of an inch from the edge. They are then turned over, and another series of holes is pierced from the other side the same distance from the first holes, but at a point of about 30° to the side towards the tail. From the first hole to the edge, a slight V-shaped cut is made, to take up some of the bulk of the board. The cords are then well pasted, the ends brought to a point, laced through the first hole, and then back through the second. The cords are drawn only tight enough to enable the boards to lie down freely without dragging at the back, and yet not so loose as to give too much play to the boards. The surplus ends of the cords are cut away almost flush, and the laced-in cords beaten down into the boards. This is done by opening the boards on to a smooth flat iron surface known as the "knocking-down iron," held firmly in the laying press, and beating both sides until the cords are almost annealed into the boards, and left quite smooth.

USE OF THE "KNOCKING-DOWN IRON"

Thin, flat, smooth tins are placed between the boards and the book, quite square with the joint; another pair are placed outside the book, with smooth wooden boards over the tins, also square with the joint; and the whole nipped together in the press very firmly, and in a perfectly true position. This latter is most essential, as the final and permanent shape of the book is now determined. A good layer of rather thin paste is laid on the back, and is allowed to stand for about 15 minutes, when the surplus paste is cleaned off with the edge of a piece of hard wood, and, finally, with a sponge or paper shavings. This serves the treble purpose of cleaning off the surface glue from the back, leaving only that which is between the sections ; the buckling over of the outer part of the section giving a perfectly smooth back : and through the moisture penetrating into the back this final moulding of the surface is made permanent when allowed to remain in the press until quite dry. This is usually allowed for overnight.

The character and preparation of the boards are matters of great importance. When most things were made with the idea of lasting indefinitely, and a monk would spend the major portion of his life in writing one book, nothing could be so suitable and so lasting as the carefully selected, suitably cut, and well-seasoned boards, frequently of oak, that were used for the protection of those beautiful vellum manuscripts. With the extension of learning, and the development of printing, grew the demand for something more ready to hand, and thus we find the boards being made of leaves of paper pasted together until the desired thickness was acquired. Being made of hand-made paper and well pasted, these made quite good boards, although not so durable as their wooden predecessors.

The development of the millboard was only a short step from this pasted board, and it was virtually little more than a very thick paper made of a similar, but generally of a harder and more durable, substance.

While varying substances have been tried in different countries and by different manufacturers, for well over a century, in England, the favoured and most durable substance so far has been the best black rope board, made chiefly from tarred rope and sail cloth. There are mills to-day still making these boards in the same manner, and with the same implements that have been in regular use since their first introduction. It is somewhat doubtful if the quality is quite so good as a generation ago, as the raw material is not so readily obtained as when there were more sailing ships, and consequently more tarred rope and sail cloth available. Still, the hand-made millboard is infinitely superior to the machine products, as the fibres in the former are so much more interwoven one with the other than in the latter product, although their component parts may be somewhat similar. The cost of the machine product is much less than the hand-made millboard, and consequently it is in more general use to-day.

A still cheaper product is the board made of straw chiefly supplied by Holland. The price and the smooth finish of this board combine to make its use by far the most common at the present day. Its durability as compared with the hand-made rope board is proportionate to the price.

For the finest bindings much consideration is given to the preparation of the hand-made boards. They are lined both sides with well-pasted paper to harden them, and give them a smooth surface. On one side there is a double lining of paper, the object of this being to draw the boards towards the book, as the pasted leather which subsequently goes on the board contracts in drying and consequently draws it outwards; but the double lining inside the board has a tendency to counteract this.

After lining the boards, it is the custom among good binders to allow them to season and harden: indeed, it has been maintained by some reputable binders that they never use a board until it has been lined and seasoned for at least two years. This may be considered unnecessary; but at least it must be granted that the boards would not suffer in the process. The millboards were originally cut in the rough with a huge pair of shears and fixed to a table or gripped in the laying press; the edges were then cut smooth and square with the plough in the same manner as the book is cut. The "plough" consists of two wooden cheeks held in position by two runners; the one cheek

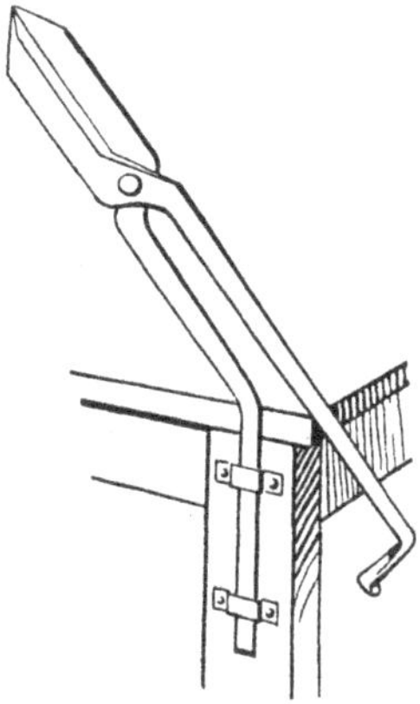

MILLBOARD SHEARS

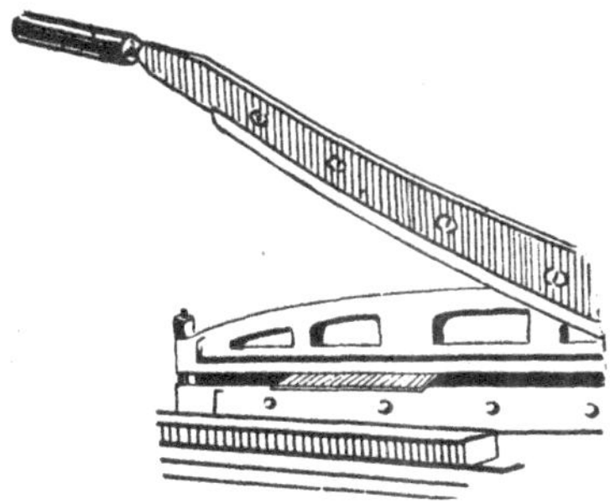

MILLBOARD CUTTER

moves between the runners, and on the left-hand side of the laying press, and the other runs freely on the other side. On the right hand is an adjustable knife running flush with the surface of the laying press. The two cheeks of the plough are closed or opened with a centre screw. The cut is made by moving the plough to and fro along the press, closing together the cheeks at each movement to make the cut. Even though millboard cutters are now used instead of the shears, the final cut is still made with the plough because of the perfect square edge obtained in this manner.

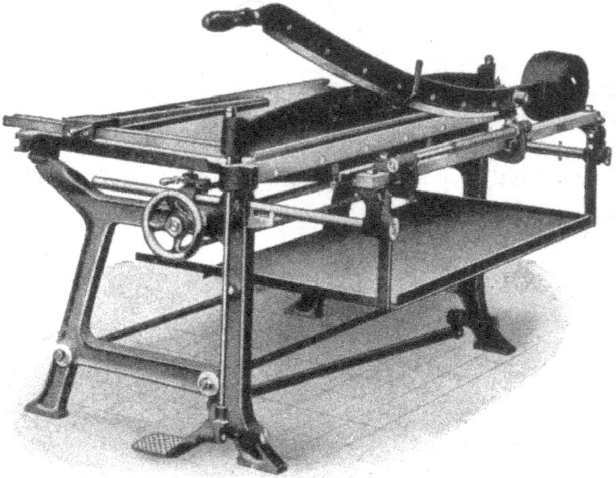

*By courtesy of* *Messrs. Krause*

HAND MILLBOARD CUTTER

*By courtesy of* *Messrs. Krause*

ROTARY MILLBOARD MACHINE

The millboard machine consists of a flat bed with a knife at one edge and another knife to cut against it on precisely the same principle as the shears. A later development for wholesale work is the rotary cutter, which, although cutting with a circular knife, still retains the principle of the shears with the two edges coming together. The development of very large and powerful guillotines has led to the frequent use of these machines for cutting boards.

# CHAPTER IX

## FORWARDING: CUTTING AND EDGE DECORATION

In considering the cutting of the book edges, it is most remarkable that, in spite of the development of huge high speed powerful three-edge cutting machines, books are still cut in-board with the plough in the same manner

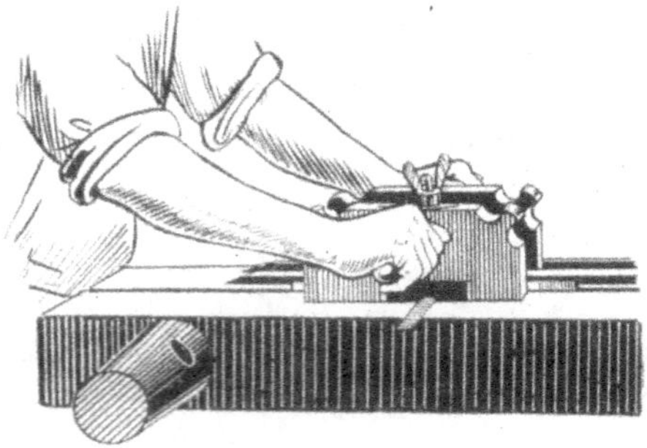

CUTTING WITH PRESS AND PLOUGH

as the monks of old cut them. Assuming the boards have been cut and squared, and the book allowed to set, it is then cut on the fore-edge. The press and plough are used in the same manner as in the cutting of the millboards; but the round in the back is first temporarily knocked out flat, after first marking the edge of the boards on the projecting ends. The boards are laid horizontally on the bench, and the book held vertically; by passing behind the back, now lying flat on the boards, two thin strips of metal at each end and carefully knocking the boards on the table, the round of the back will come out. The book is then held between a pair of cutting boards, and fixed in the laying press.

The " cutting boards " are wedge-shaped and similar to the backing boards, only the base has equal angles with the sides. On the right hand the cutting board is flush with the cheek of the press, and the line of the board marked on the end paper is just the distance above that will represent the square of the book. On the left-hand side the cutting board is exactly in alignment with the mark on the end paper, and exactly the distance of a square above the press. That is to say, the two lines on the book representing the edges of the boards are both above the press the desired height of the squares, held between two cutting boards, the right-hand one being flush with the press, the other a square above, and the back remaining perfectly flat. The book is then cut in the same manner as the boards, the knife being kept particularly sharp. When removed from the press the back will automatically fall back into its round, and the straight cut made on the fore-edge will give a concave shape the exact reverse of the back. The head and tail are similarly treated but minus the cutting boards, and without interfering with the round of the back. For the head the right-hand board is dropped a square and the left one raised a square above the press, the back being towards the cut, i.e. away from the operator if he makes

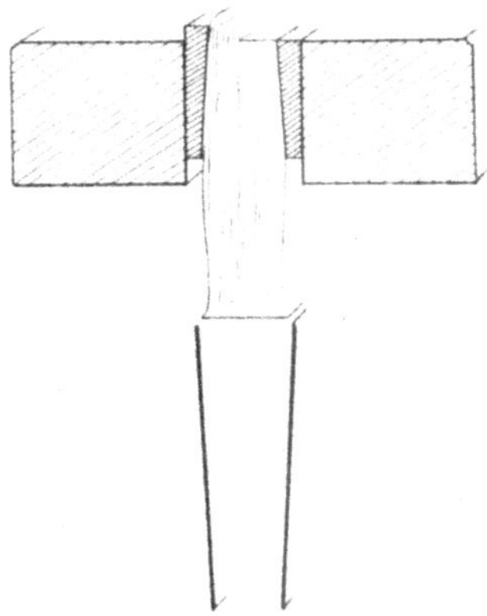

CUTTING FORE-EDGE IN BOARDS

the cut towards him. As a precautionary measure against cutting into the board, a waste piece of thin board is placed between the book and the left-hanp board. The book is turned round and the tail cut in the same way.

To the craftsman who loves his craft it is a matter of extreme regret that the practice of this form of in-board work grows more and more limited each day. The care and skill necessary to produce a perfect

*By courtesy of Messrs. Krause*

THREE-EDGE CUTTER

*By courtesy of Messrs. Krause*

GUILLOTINE

in-board book are becoming less appreciated to-day than a generation ago, and so the method is slowly but surely dying out.

Usually nowadays, the book is taken after it is sewn and put through the nipping machine, to get all the swelling out of the back. A considerable number of books are taken together, placed to two gauges on the guillotine, when with a touch of a lever the knife comes down cutting the fore-edge, and as it returns two parallel knives come down at right angles and cut head and tail. The books are rounded after the cutting, and a comparison of the fore-edges will show the difference in the two methods at once. The one cut before rounding will usually show steps in the fore-edge whilst the fore-edge of the in-board book will be perfectly smooth.

All sorts of modifications of these two extremes may be made. The fore-edge may be cut without taking the swelling out of the back, and the craftsman may rely on his skill of handling in the process of rounding, to minimize

*By courtesy of Messrs. Smyth-Horne, Ltd.*

THREE-EDGE CUTTER

the danger of steps in the fore-edge. He may then attach his boards, and cut head and tail afterwards, either with the plough or in the single knife guillotine; or he may cut, round, then cut head and tail, subsequently attaching the boards. The large wholesale binderies do not attach their boards until after the cover is made.

It is interesting to note that many valuable old books of about a century ago are cut in very close to the print, in fact, they are very often bled. The term "bled" is used to denote that the letterpress or plates have been cut into. The poor binders of that day have been unmercifully execrated by book-collectors for this sacrilege. In extenuation it may be pleaded that by the sale of these cuttings the binder paid his rent, and it was his necessity to make the weight of shavings as big as possible to meet this charge that he cut deeply, for the payment he received for his binding was scarcely an existence. The collectors would be more fair if they saddled the binder's clientele with at least some of the blame. To-day, the pendulum has swung, and we have the fetish of the uncut edge. Without questioning the aesthetic merit of the uncut edge, it is found even at the present day that the books are being ruined by dust and atmospheric action through the looseness of this edge. For utility books, an uncut edge is inconvenient to open, and for books intended to be kept indefinitely they are unwise, as dust and decay enter through them.

A cut edge, especially if gilt, affords a great protection to the interior of a book and is certainly much easier for reference. At the same time, for a book on beautiful hand-made paper with deckle edges to be cut would amount to sacrilege from the artistic point of view, and on a par with murder from the collector's standpoint. But even then the uncut edge generally requires a little tidying. The variation in sizes in hand-made paper will sometimes give a single leaf a projection of half an inch beyond its fellows, in which case even a collector might tolerate the cutting of a little of that. There is a degree between the uncut and the cut edge that is known as the trimmed edge. This is so elastic that it may mean anything according to the conscience of the binder, the requirements of his clients, or the value of the book itself. A book may be cut before sewing, the subsequent sewing giving a disturbance of the edge which may pass as a trimmed edge. The more generally accepted trimmed edge is that which is trimmed section by section in the millboard machine, or by knife and straight-edge.

An excellent trimming machine has been in use for many years which trims the book after it has been sewn. The book is fixed on to a moving bed and the projecting

*By courtesy of* *Messrs. Smyth-Horne, Ltd.*

THE SEYBOLD CONTINUOUS AUTOMATIC BOOK TRIMMER

part of the edge runs against a quickly revolving knife, giving very satisfactory results. A more recent development on a similar principle is the continuous moving bed, which carries a succession of books past the knife as quickly as the operator can feed it.

The decoration of the cut edge has occupied the attention of the binder in many different ways for centuries past. The most generally adopted method is the plain gilt edge. The process, though simple in technique, requires great skill to accomplish satisfactorily. The book is held tightly in the laying press, and the edge very evenly scraped with an ordinary steel scraper, a mixture of powdered blacklead and glaire is made into a thick paste, a thin coating laid on the edge, and thoroughly brushed until quite dry. The glaire is made by adding the white of one egg to a teacupful of water, the whole being well beaten up and allowed to stand overnight, and then strained off. The gold leaf is cut into convenient sizes to suit the particular edge, picked up on a piece of thin paper, and laid ready to hand. It will be found that, if the paper has been previously rubbed over the hair or cheek, it will have picked up sufficient grease to enable the gold to cling temporarily. With a fairly large brush a generous layer of size is run over the edge, and the gold leaf laid on the wet size immediately, and allowed to dry. According to the temperature this will take from twenty to sixty minutes. If allowed to get too dry, the subsequent burnishing will not be so satisfactory; if not dry enough, the gold will rub off. The edge is rubbed over with the burnisher, at first with a thin paper over it to set the gold, then with the flat burnisher direct. The pressure on the burnisher at first is very light, but is increased each time it is gone over until the desired results are obtained. A little beeswax on a piece of very soft leather gently rubbed over the surface is of very great assistance when burnishing. A flat blood-stone gives the best results. For gilding the fore-edge, the back is knocked up flat as in the cutting, for what is termed plain gilding; but for solid gilding, it is gilt in the round. If the paper of the book is deficient in size, a good coat of vellum size is given at the outset; if there is too much size, as in art paper, the glaire used must be thinner; even water is sufficient sometimes. In such cases a very useful precaution is to fan out the leaves before starting, and dust with French chalk to minimize the possibility of the leaves sticking. It will be fairly obvious that the gilding of a fore-edge in the round calls for much greater skill in manipulation than gilding on the flat. To lessen the difficulty of coping with the concave, half the edge is laid on at a time, and this from the middle to the edge. The scraping, gilding, and burnishing being done while the book is in the round, the edge acquires a perfectly solid appearance, much approved of by some, and greatly disliked by others. The dislike is an aesthetic one, and so may the approval be ; but the advantage is that the solid edge is a more perfect protection for the paper. Whatever may be said against the gilt edges from an artistic point of view, it is the most successful method of treating the edges as a protection for the book itself. It will resist atmospheric action and the penetration of dust better than any other. " Dull gilt edges " are only burnished through paper, and " rough gilt edges " are gilt before the book is sewn.

With varying degrees of success, binders have from time to time added decoration to the gilt edges by impressing with small engraved tools made slightly hot various designs almost without limit in character, the tools used being the same as those employed for decorating the cover. These tooled edges are known as " gauffered edges," and perhaps the most successful are those made up of dots. Colour is sometimes introduced into the scheme of decoration, by first scraping the parts to be coloured. A very favourite method with some binders is to make a symmetrically geometric design with definitely balanced shapes on which very delicate miniatures are painted. One method possibly more popular for its mystifying effect than its artistic merit, is to fan out the fore-edge on which a picture is painted, and then gild the edge afterwards. The painting disappears when the book is closed and reappears when it is fanned out. A very common method of treating the edges, more in vogue a generation ago than it is to-day, was to marble them in the same manner as the paper is marbled. This was invariably done to match the pattern of the end paper.

Plain-coloured edges have been adopted for many centuries in almost every conceivable shade: reds and yellows being most in evidence. The most common of all is the sprinkled edge. Commercially it is the simplest and cheapest, and it gives sufficient colour to take off the blank coldness of the plain white edge. For lending library bindings this method is generally considered most satisfactory. Various tricks are resorted to for the sprinkling, but maybe the most efficient method is with the ærograph. Different effects are sometimes obtained by previously throwing on the edge grains of rice, bread-crumbs, tobacco, or sundry other things, then sprinkling over them. The effect is artistic or otherwise according to individual fancy.

There is one more feature to be considered before entering on the question of covers for the book, and that is "the head-band." This band at the head and tail of the book was originally made when the book was sewn. It consisted of a cord or leather thong similar to the ordinary bands, and when the threads came out at the ends of the book they were twisted round this band. The ends were laced in the boards similarly to the rest. This lacing-in necessitated cutting the cover at a vital point, and the strength gained was largely counterbalanced by the weakening of the cover. Wisely or not this method has fallen into disuse, and in its place a headband is sewn on after the book has been forwarded. This has developed into quite an elaborate piece of work calling for much skill and judgment in the manipulation of the fine silks sometimes used, and the blending of their colours.

These headbands are worked on strips of vellum, cane, leather or cord. The depth is just a fraction less than the size of the squares, so that, when the silk is twisted round and the turn in of the cover brought over, the combined height is the same as the square when covered. If the headband is being worked in one colour only, the boards are set back flush with the edge, the book being held in the press across the bottom corner at an angle of 45° with the fore-edge facing the operator. The needle is threaded, and the silk knotted on to it, and passed down through the middle of the first section below the kettle-stitch, leaving about a third of the silk sticking out of the book. The needle is passed through the same hole again, leaving a loop through which the strip of vellum or other medium is passed; the loop is then drawn tight and the headband held fast at the left-hand side. For convenience of handling, the headband is cut about half as long again as the width of the book, and may be supported at the outset by placing a needle behind it at the right-hand side. The needle end of the silk is brought over the headband and twisted round the other end of the silk left projecting out of the book; it is then taken round the headband and again twisted round the other. This is repeated a few times, and then the needle is passed again into the book at the section immediately under it, and brought out below the kettle-stitch, and so on to the end, repeating the ties as often as necessary, and finishing off with a double knot at the end.

Two colours may be worked by knotting them together, leaving one colour projecting and the other forming the loop; these are alternated in the twisting round the headband, and may be done in series as desired. The same applies to a multiple of colours, with which an infinite variety of effects may be obtained. The ends of the headband are cut close to the silk, and the length is made just a fraction short of the width of the book to allow for the setting of the head when covered. The tail is then worked in a similar manner. These are known as "worked headbands." There are also many varieties of headbands which are most effective, being made by machinery in long lengths on to a material which can be stuck on to the back of the book. Sometimes their effect almost equals the worked headbands; but for durability they are not to be compared with them. It may be interesting to mention here that the skill and dexterity of some headbanders are so remarkable, that one at least has been known to work with human hair instead of silk, the combination of very light and very dark hair being quite pleasing. The supply of material being limited by the reluctance of ladies to part with what was then considered their crowning glory, the fact that this unique headband is not being imitated is perhaps accounted for; and with the bobs and shingles of the present day there is little likelihood of its being revived, as it would be difficult to gather from the workshop sufficient material for even one little book.

# CHAPTER X

## COVERING

FOR covering books, many different materials have been used with more or less success. Among the most serviceable coverings to stand the test of time are the old monastic bindings in vellum and pigskin. It would be fallacious, however, to conclude that these particular leathers, if used to-day, would give like results.

While it cannot be denied that the original nature of the skin must play an important part in a test of durability, yet it must not be forgotten that the form of manufacture is of still greater import.

In making a comparison between modern sheepskin and modern pigskin, the sheepskin in any of its multitude of forms is not to be compared with pigskin, either for durability or for anything else. Yet the sheepskin coverings of a couple of centuries ago will still outlast many of our modern pigskin covers. Neither the leather manufacturers nor the binders are wholly to blame for this. The demand for perfectly unblemished, delicate, and evenly coloured skins, coupled with commercial exigencies, have compelled the manufacturers to produce an artificial material from a natural product to the detriment of all concerned. Still it cannot be denied that some of the modern products are admirable, and it is to be hoped that posterity may find some of the fears expressed for the modern leather groundless.

In determining the best kind of leather to use, due consideration must be given to the subsequent purpose of the book. A book destined to stand on the shelf and only be very occasionally referred to, may be suitably covered in vellum, but for a flexibly sewn book made to open very freely, and meant for constant use, such as a dictionary, morocco makes by far the more suitable covering.

The nomenclature of modern leathers is often difficult to follow, many manufacturers adopting for them names of their own choosing which may mean anything. For about half a century, one of the leathers most favoured by the best binders has been morocco. All moroccos are made from goatskins; but all goatskins are not necessarily morocco. Moroccos vary considerably in quality, and for fine richly tooled bindings perhaps the most popular of recent years is that known as "French Cape Levant Morocco." One naturally expects something exceptional from a leather that takes its name from so many remote parts of the globe, and opinion is fairly uniform as to the handsome character and appearance of this leather. It is made from the skin of a very large Cape goat, with a big grain known as Levant grain, as distinct from the smaller pin-head grain of the ordinary morocco. It is generally considered that the French give the best finish to the leather for bookbinding purposes; hence the composite name. One notable feature of this leather is the fact that it crushes and polishes well without losing the large deep grain which is its chief distinction. It is comparatively mellow and kind for paring and covering books. Hard-grain morocco appears to be made from different kinds of goats. The grain is about the shape and size of a pin's head, and many of these moroccos are very durable. Maybe the least durable is the kind known as "Persian morocco," due chiefly to the original character of the skins. When these moroccos are covering the book it is difficult to distinguish them with any degree of certainty.

For some years past, much discussion has centred round the manufacture of leathers for bookbinding purposes, and honest attempts have been made to produce acid-free morocco of which time alone will prove the efficacy. Despite all efforts to the contrary, it has been found that certain combinations of dyes will, in themselves, set up acid action, and so nullify all precautionary measures. A leather increasing in popularity among a certain clientele is the Niger morocco, wholly produced by the natives of Nigeria. Its toughness, flexibility, and freedom from acids make its durability almost a certainty, while its texture and colouring are most artistic. Another morocco more popular a century ago, and much favoured by Roger Payne, is the straight-grained morocco, with its lines all running in one direction—durable in those days, but the artificially produced grain of to-day does not make for popularity among binders on the look-out for lasting qualities. Cross-grained morocco, with its diagonally crossed lines, shares the same fate.

Much as calf has been decried of late years, it still retains a certain amount of favour for light, dainty books. Its fragility is the chief burden of complaint against it ; and this is probably due to the treatment it receives rather than to the character of the skin. Many calf bindings of the seventeenth century are still quite sound, but it is doubtful if these skins were either dressed or coloured in any way. The rich tone they possess to-day is most likely the result of the mellowing action of time. The later calf bindings which preceded the introduction of coloured or dyed calf have not stood the ravages of time so well, chiefly because the binders, dissatisfied with the raw unfinished character of the covers, set about staining them. Two of the chief ingredients used for this purpose were salts of tartar and copperas—the former not helpful, and the latter positively harmful. With these two and a few less harmful vegetable stains, all manner of sprinkles, mottles, marbles, and stains were produced, all more or less charming in appearance.

The famous hand-stained "Bedford bindings" were produced from what is known as "fair calf" (a simple bark-tanned calf in an almost raw state), washed over frequently with a weak solution of salts of tartar, and exposed to the light. It is stated that the gradual process of staining these covers took six months. Sprinkling was done with the splashes of a brush tapped against a press pin, or by rubbing over a sieve a stiff brush charged with either salts of tartar or copperas. Rubbing over a sieve gave a fine sprinkle, and the splashes a coarse one. The salts of tartar gave a warm brown toned sprinkle, the copperas a grey, and the two in conjunction, a good black.

The Cambridge "pane sides" were produced by laying a panel of paper on the sides during the sprinkling process, leaving a light panel when the paper was removed from the page. "Mottling" was generally done with a coarse sponge dabbed on the side. All these, with the addition of various little tricks of individual workmen, resulted in a goodly variety of effects.

"Tree marbling" was done by bending the board down the middle, tilting the book at a sharp angle, and throwing on the splashes of salts of tartar and copperas, quickly followed by coarse splashes of water sufficient to make the main combined splashes run towards the middle and the bottom of the board, giving the branching effect so familiar and once so popular. Following the introduction of coloured or dyed calf, these methods began to fall into disuse, and to-day they are the exception rather than the rule, although still used, chiefly for period bindings.

Among the names given to sheepskins the best known are : " basil," " roan," and " skiver." Sheepskin lends itself to imitation of every kind of leather imaginable. One may see crushed Levant morocco imitated so as to deceive all but the expert, and often the thickness not more than thin paper, and more than likely not so strong as some paper. Most of the wholesale leather bindings are in sheepskin and look remarkably well, pleasing a clientele which apparently derives satisfaction from possessing a leather binding, regardless of the fact that it may not last very long. Some are in lambskin beautifully decorated, and nothing could be more dainty ; but there its merit stops. For a little book of poems seldom if ever read, these covers are nice so long as they are kept in the box sold with them. For a dictionary or book for use, cloth is far superior.

The character of vellum seems to have changed but little during the centuries in which it has been in use, but here again the nomenclature is misleading. Vellum, as its name denotes, comes from the same source as veal, and was originally made of calfskins. To-day, the manufacturers quote us: "goat vellums" and "sheep vellums," so the original name is losing its significance. The real vellum shows no sign of grain whatever, the sheep vellum shows slight indications of one, while the goat vellum has quite a pronounced grain. Parchment is made from thinner, or split sheepskins.

Pigskin is so well known for its strength and lasting qualities that one would be inclined to head the list with it. For bookbinding it is most suitable for large books ; but of recent years it has lost much of its popularity owing to its not being so flexible as could be desired. In its more natural state it is too greasy to hold satisfactorily as a cover, and if degreased it loses much of its strength and charm.

Cowhide is generally too hard and inflexible for any but very large books. Russia leather is, however, made from cowhide, and for some years was greatly in demand for the finest bindings. Time has proved its undoing as, unless constantly handled, it perishes very quickly. Regular and frequent handling is good for any leather, but it is necessary to the very existence of a Russia binding. Fine sealskin makes a very beautiful covering for books, and should give lasting wear if not too much punished in course of manufacture. The larger antique grained seals make very handsome bindings, but they are not over popular with the binder owing to the extreme difficulty of paring them. The poor binder who pares his leather by hand almost despairs before he has his cover ready, as he finds the edge of his knife almost gone after the first cut.

Every kind of skin imaginable has been tried for the binding of books, but the use of the more exceptional skins has been for the sake of novelty rather than utility. Even human skin has been used, but there the novelty becomes gruesome.

After leather, the next most important covering for books is bookbinder's cloth. It was very early in the nineteenth century when cloth, as we know it to-day, was first used for bookbinding, and, if statistics could be obtained, it would be interesting to know how many millions of yards of this material are now used weekly by the great English-speaking nations alone, little more than a century from its introduction. Although much advance has been made in variety of character and colour, it is questionable if proportionate advance has been made in durability, for many of the original cloth bindings are still quite sound, and yet show signs of good use. Perhaps the most outstanding material of this class is the linen buckram that is superseding leather in many public libraries, and is noted for what appears to be its almost imperishable character. Lack of flexibility makes its use undesirable for very frequently used books, but, for books for occasional reference, it is most suitable. Still more recent years have seen the introduction of imitation leather cloths such as Rexine, Pluviusin, and the like, claiming enormous strength, durability, and insect-resisting qualities for tropical and semi-tropical climates. Silk, satin, and velvet are occasionally used for covering books ; but these are generally purely fancy coverings with very little utility.

Both book and cover require some attention before the covering can be done. The back of the book may require some lining. Most books of average size and thickness are improved with a covering of mull over the back. This mull is a very openly woven material which gives support to the back and yet enables the cover to grip direct on to the paper of the book. For books sewn flexibly, or books designed to have very flexible backs, it is usually advisable to have nothing but the leather direct on the back. If the headbands are worked, most binders like to put a strip of brown paper head and tail to give support to them. When this is done the brown paper should be split off when nearly dry, and sand-papered down leaving only sufficient fibre to hold the headband and its ties in position. For calf books (or books requiring much decoration on the back) that have been sewn in the ordinary way, it is usual to make a hollow back. This hollow is made by first glueing on to the back a piece of good quality brown, or other paper, rubbing it well down to assure its sticking perfectly, and setting the headband firmly to it. A second lining is put on over this, but the paper is left an indefinite width. When the back is well glued this paper is laid flush with the joint on the left-hand side, rubbed down well, creased over the full width of the back, then quickly drawn off, and, while the glue is fresh, the paper is folded back on itself with the glued side uppermost. The glued side is then folded over, giving three thicknesses of brown paper the exact width of the back, of which two only are stuck together, leaving a hollow space between. The back is again well glued and this hollow lining stuck into position. According to the width of the back and the substance of the paper, so the number of layers of paper is determined. Two linings on the back and two off is the general rule for an average octavo book.

Different workmen have different methods of making this hollow, but the results are about the same. What may be open to question is the principle of the hollow back itself. It certainly has the advantage of keeping the back of the book nice especially when it is a smooth, finely-finished leather. Experience shows that, while hollow-backed books of a past generation may perish in the joints, causing the backs to come away altogether, other books of a similar period and material, but with fast backs, not only perish in the joints, but, if they are much used, the whole back will be broken and perished also and probably will crumble away completely. Whatever may be urged against the hollow back, one must admit that it is much more readily repaired, and it is to be feared that the next generation will have much repairing to do if they desire to preserve some of the bindings of to-day.

If bands are to be used on these hollow backs, they may be either strips of leather or cord, and they are stuck on the back of the hollow. By those who object to hollow backs, they are referred to as " false bands " ;

while to those who are not adverse to this type of back the chief value of these bands is an aesthetic one.

For " case books," the lining of the back consists of a piece of mull stuck to the back but projecting almost an inch on to the end papers. This is called the first lining ; the second lining consists of a piece of paper almost the size of the back stuck on over that. In this case the hollow is obtained by putting a strip of paper on the cover and pasting down the ends only.

For the bound book three other points have to be considered before actually covering. A little piece is nipped off the board along the joint and against the headbands. For a crown octavo, the distance down the joint is about a quarter of an inch, and the distance in from the back about an eighth on the outside, to a sixteenth on the inside. This is known as " back cornering." Its utility value is not very apparent ; but its effect on the setting of the head when covered is a very superior finish, and it probably does take up some of the strain off the turn-in of the leather at this point. Another item is the slitting down the hollow of the lined-up book to enable the cover to be turned in inside the hollow. Finally, the slips on which the boards are laced are well pasted at the point from the first hole to the back, the squares set exact, the slips well rubbed down and not disturbed from that position until the back has been drawn on.

The preparation of the cover is a matter of exceptional skill, if it is of good solid leather. The cover is cut from the skin about three-quarters of an inch larger all round for an octavo book, and the position of the boards and back marked on the inside of the cover with soft pencil. Its thickness and flexibility are considered in relation to the size of the book. A full-thickness Levant morocco cover may require to be reduced to less than half its thickness ; and it is still the practice in some places to do this with a paring knife. Paring knives have almost as much varied individuality as the workmen. Perhaps the most generally favoured is the French one, with a blade about 1½ in. wide, and 4 in. or 5 in. long, cut nearly square at the end, perfectly flat on the underside, and a good, long bevel at the other. This knife should be made of the finest steel, and the cutting edge, which is at the end, kept as sharp as a razor. A lithographer's stone is the best surface to pare on. The cut

USE OF THE PARING KNIFE

is made away from the operator, a very little being taken off at a time. A very gradual reduction of thickness is made from the mark where the edge of the board will be to the edge of the leather, and possibly a reduction of thickness may be necessary at the part covering the back.

Since the introduction of the "Fortuna" paring machine, much of this hard and skilled work has been done away with. The principle of the Fortuna is that the leather is carried under a foot adjusted to the required thickness, against a swiftly revolving cylindrical knife, kept constantly sharp against a grinding wheel. For the edge of the leather, the adjustment of the foot will give any degree of bevel required. A little dressing of the surface by hand is sometimes necessary afterward; and this is most effectively done with a spoke-shave, like the one used by carpenters, the leather being clamped to the stone at the edge.

A buffing machine, consisting of a swiftly revolving roller covered with glass-paper, is another very effective and expeditious method of dressing the surface after the paring machine. The possibilities of purchasing leather shaved, or split by the manufacturers to any desired thickness, minimizes the cost of covering, but it is to be feared that the covers of many beautifully neat books are shaved to a point of real injury, and are only charming covers void of substance. For real serviceability, it is always advisable to select covers of a natural thickness, that will be suitable to the individual book with as little paring as possible.

For bound books, pure flour paste is the best medium for sticking the covers on. The covers should be well pasted, and allowed to stand folded in half with the pasted sides together for five or ten minutes, or until the paste has made the covers soft and pliable. One side of the book is laid on the cover in its exact position, the cover drawn over the back, and laid on the other side. The book is stood on its fore-edges with the projecting turn-in thrown out, while the leather is moulded over the back between the bands. This must be done with the minimum of stretching; in fact, the whole covering must be done with the idea of not stretching the leather; for in drying, shrinkage will take place and produce almost insuperable difficulties by drawing the boards into all manner of shapes. The softer flank parts of the leather will yield more readily than will the harder parts near the backbone, and the shrinkage will be irregular if drawn too tightly.

Before the edges are turned in, the corners of the

leather are cut away at an angle of 45° with the edge, and crossing the corner of the boards at a point the thickness of the board distant from that corner, the cut being at a very long angle. The fore-edges are then turned in, and, if a true start and a true angle cut has been made, it should result in a perfect mitre. The edges are next turned in at the head and tail strictly flush with the boards, but enough is left over the head-bands to turn over on to them to the extent of almost the thickness of the boards. In turning over the leather near the joint, the tendency should be toward the joint, in order to avoid any strain when the board is opened.

There is a little piece on the edge of each corner requiring careful treatment for neatness. Some coverers turn in this piece on itself before turning over the fore-edge, others draw it over and close it into itself at the point of mitre; while some do not cut the corner piece away until after turning in; then they cut the corner off with the shears, laying down one end over the other, cutting right through the two at a true mitre line, and removing the underneath piece, thus butting the two edges together. This latter may be neat, but the shrinkage in the drying frequently leaves a little gap, causing a weakness at an essential point. The over-lapping of the ordinary method, if skilfully handled, is much more successful both in appearance and service-ability.

The boards are then opened right back and set square in the joint, each separately, and then carefully closed again. A thread is passed round the book between the back and the sides, pressing in the leather at the back cornering, and tied in position. With a fine-pointed folder the head is set over the headbands, by moulding the mellow leather into the desired shape. The leather will now be in a condition to set nicely into the bands.

This may be done with a band-stick pressed over them, or by band-nippers, both answering the purpose; perhaps the band-nippers most effectively if skilfully used. The band-stick is a long, narrow stick, with a groove cut out the width of the band. The band-nippers are pliers with a long flat edge, and may be opened or closed to any desired width.

Oiled boards are placed between the book and the cover to prevent the moisture of the turn-in from injuring the book. Small books may be allowed to dry standing on their fore-edges, but large ones should at least be allowed to set, before standing them up finally to dry.

Case books, i.e. books that do not have the boards laced in, are turned in off the book. The boards are temporarily held in position, the cover drawn over, the boards released, and the cover treated quite flat, and allowed to dry in that position. For quantities of the same size, a register is taken of the width of the back, and the whole cover made apart from the book. In cases of this kind it is the general custom to glue the boards, lay them into position, and paste the turn-in afterwards. For cloth, buckram, and the like, glue is generally used throughout.

Truly marvellous machines have been invented for making these cloth cases. A roll of cloth passes over a glued roller, arms with suction points lift the boards, and place them in true position on the glued material. A knife cuts the cloth to size, other devices turn in the edges, and the cases pass along to meet the book at some other stage almost as fast as one can count.

It is difficult to lay down any particular rule as to when paste or glue should be used: the nature of the work and material must determine that. It is generally necessary to line vellum with paper before covering, and then cover

*By courtesy of* *Messrs. Smyth-Horne, Ltd.*

AUTOMATIC CASE-MAKING MACHINE, MAKING 10–12 PER MINUTE

*By courtesy of* *The T. W. & C. B. Sheridan Co., Ltd*

AUTOMATIC CASE-MAKING MACHINE, MAKING 2,000 PER HOUR.

with paste. With silk, it is inadvisable to do more than stick down the turn-in, leaving the sides loose ; and perhaps the best medium for making silk stick is gelatine. Many limp lambskins and other light leathers are covered loose. This gives extreme flexibility, and leaves

*By courtesy of Messrs. Smyth-Horne, Ltd.*

A CASING-IN MACHINE

the finely finished surface of the leather entirely undisturbed. In the case of padded sides the pads are usually slipped under the cover after turning in. The padding is held between stiff smooth paper which is pulled away after the pad is in position.

Half-bound books, i.e. books with leather backs and corners, are treated in the same way as full bindings, the corners usually being stuck on first. The price generally determines the width of the back ; but a good guide for

*By courtesy of The T. W. & C. B. Sheridan Co., Ltd.*

MACHINE FOR APPLYING ADHESIVE TO THE EDGES OF LEATHER CASES BEFORE TURNING IN.

*By courtesy of The T. W. & C. B. Sheridan Co., Ltd.*

MACHINE FOR TURNING IN THE EDGES OF LEATHER CASES.

proportion is for the width of the leather on the side to be almost one-third of the width of the whole side, and the same distance for the triangle at the corner, measuring from the hypotenuse to the apex, the sides of the triangle being equal. The sides of these books may be equally well of paper or cloth. Half-bound books are a great economy, as the shape of the skin makes for so much waste in cutting out square covers, whereas the corners will cut well into the flanks.

The pasting down of a bound book calls for some careful consideration. The protection leaf in front of the end paper is carefully torn away, and all paper and glue or paste in the joint cleaned away without injuring the leather. The end paper is lifted up into the position it will finally remain in, well squared in the joint. The fore-edge will fall shorter than the head and tail on the board, and this is rectified by marking an even width all round, and trimming the paper round with knife and straight-edge on a cutting tin. The end paper is then pasted, drawn over into position, and well rubbed down, especially in the joint, when it is allowed to dry in this position. With case books, one end paper is pasted, placed in position on its board, and then the other end is pasted and the other board pulled over into position, and the whole allowed to dry in the press.

## CHAPTER XI

### FINISHING: (I) ITS HISTORICAL DEVELOPMENT

It is necessary only to consult the bibliography of book decoration for one to realize that the subject is an inexhaustible one. New facts appertaining to its history and the individuals concerned in making it, are constantly being brought to light. New ideals and new expressions are for ever springing up, making the subject bristle with life and controversy. Much that was done in its earlier stages, can hardly be claimed as bookbinder's work. Benvenuto Cellini lent his genius to the decoration of at least one book; but no bookbinder would dare to claim him as a fellow-craftsman on that count. Much of the very early decoration was the work of the goldsmith, the jeweller, the workers in ivory and enamels, and the embroiderer. The absorbing interest and extreme beauty of some of this extraneous work can only be dealt with exclusively or in relation to its own craft; only when one arrives at the decoration on the leather actually covering the book can the binder fairly claim that the decoration wholly belongs to his craft.

Although the decorative treatment of leather has been very varied, the making of impressions on its surface has been the chief mode of decorative expression from the birth of the leather-covered book to the present day. Some very interesting incunabula of the fifteenth century have repeating ornamental devices stamped on their pigskin covers. Of those produced in England but few remain to us, many having been destroyed at the time of the Reformation; but from Germany and the Netherlands there are fine examples of this and earlier work still extant. The ornament of these stamps, probably made of metal, was cut in the flat surface. The small stamps were hammered on to the wet yielding surface of the leather, and the large ones were pressed in with the aid of the laying press. Lines were made by wheels of varying widths of line, and often the repeating ornaments were made by cutting the design on the surface of a broad wheel, and impressing that on the leather. Thus we have the fillet for the lines, and the much despised roll for the continuous or repeating ornaments; both tools still in regular use at the present day.

The ornament being cut from the flat surface became raised when impressed on the leather by forcing down the background. To-day, these impressions are referred to as "blind tooling" in contradistinction to "gold tooling." Historians do not appear to have been able to establish with any degree of certainty the beginning of gold tooling, but there is little doubt that Aldus, in Italy, can lay claim to having developed it in Europe to a very high state of perfection. The style of ornament he used was distinctly Eastern in character, and it is more than probable that the technique was Eastern also. For centuries previous, the Persians had produced some magnificent bindings, where gold and colour were freely used; perhaps the finest of all being almost contemporary with Aldus. In the earlier Persian work, the gold and colour were both undoubtedly painted in the stamped impressions; but the later examples are of such a character as to make one almost certain that the gold was impressed with hot tools; and most certainly with consummate skill. But, for the real beginning of gilt decoration on leather, it is necessary to go farther back than the Persians, for in their earliest work there are evidences of strong Chinese influence, and, once the historic element becomes involved in the antiquity of China, it is lost in a maze of intricacy. One can only give each age its due merit for its share in the development of this beautiful art.

From the time of Aldus we have a fairly clear record of its development, and can give to each individual his meed of praise for his part in its progress. While Aldus was strongly influenced by prevailing Eastern work, he was not by any means a copyist. He had a style distinctly his own, and his geometrical frame work was beautifully proportioned, giving a feeling of fine stability and restraint.

Grolier, while resident in Italy as French Ambassador, was strongly influenced by the work of his friend, Aldus,

and developed a style of geometrical interlaced work interwoven with scrolls, their terminals and branches of ornamental foliage being very similar to the oriental character favoured by Aldus. The geometrical work, although intricate, never lost dignity and repose. The terminals were frequently given added richness by having parallel lines across them; latterly known as azured on account of their heraldic counterpart. On his return to France he still retained the character of his work, and, although it is impossible definitely to establish the identity of the designers he employed, it would be quite safe to assume that he exercised a great personal influence over them, if he did not actually design his work himself ; as, right to the end, although he never lacked variety, he was most consistent in his style of pure and restrained magnificence.

The inaccuracy of some of the geometric detail favours the suggestion that the workman who tooled the books did not conceive the geometric interlacement. It is impossible to pass this great bibliophile without a word for his fine noble character so clearly indicated in the motto on his books, "Io Grolierii et Amicorum," which speaks more eloquently than anything that can be written about him.

Maioli, the contemporary of Grolier, was evidently much influenced by his style while retaining much of his own individuality. One of the most distinguishing characteristics of this great bibliophile is the fact that his Arabic terminals were frequently in outline, in contradistinction to the azure of Grolier and the solid of Aldus. His interlaced work was less severely geometrical, and in places became rather floreated ; but, with all its ornateness, it never lacked dignity and stability.

From this time onward most of the history of tooled bookbinding was confined to France. She led the Western World in this beautiful craft, and the work of all other countries for more than a century was but a very feeble reflection of her magnificent achievements. An artistic aristocracy fostering the art of an artistic people, this beautiful craft could not help flourishing in such fruitful soil.

It is generally admitted that during the reign of Henri II the highest point of perfection was reached.

Much fine work was done for the King himself, and his beautiful mistress, Dianne de Poytiers, by an unknown binder. This binder had a distinctive style of his own, generally much more elaborate and florid than that of his contemporaries, but none the less well balanced and restrained and with an unequalled perfection of technique.

Nicholas Eve and his son, Clovis, followed with another style, mainly composed of well-balanced geometrical compartments filled with a variety of floreated scroll work.

In the next century perhaps the most outstanding style was that known by the name of " Le Gascon," an unknown personality sometimes identified with the name of Florimond Badier. The chief distinctive characteristic of this style was the fine dotted scrolls frequently enclosed in geometrical shapes not far removed from the Eve style that preceded it.

In the eighteenth century the family of Padeloup marked a distinctive style mainly characterized by its inlays of coloured leathers of diapered simple geometrical form, devoid of any floreation. The Derome family, in the same century, mainly confined their ornament to symmetrical corner tooling of a very richly engraved floreated scroll work, pertaining very closely to the rococo style of the Louis period.

Perhaps it would be unwise to make invidious distinctions between the more modern binders of France, but Marius Michel and his son have developed a style so distinctive, that it is almost impossible to pass it over without mention. The designs are often based on natural forms with an expression of breadth and simplicity, at the same time bold and restrained, giving a feeling of complete satisfaction and charm. The ornament is generally expressed in colour, outlined in blind, and very often without the use of gold at all.

In England there has been little to boast of in the way of decorative binding. Much has been said of the Mearne bindings of the seventeenth century, but although not without merit, and certainly distinctive in character, they were lacking in stability and proportion. In the latter part of the eighteenth century, that erratic and rather dissipated genius, Roger Payne, stands out perhaps as the greatest, if not the only, bookbinder to

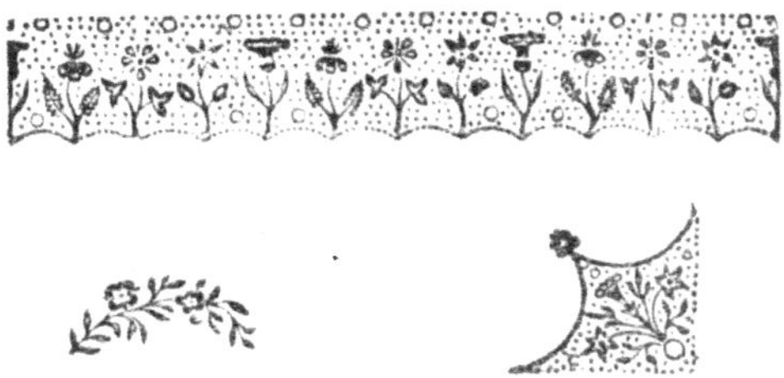

develop a style in England, entirely original and yet of a very high standard of decorative merit.

Probably because he was too poor to do otherwise, he frequently cut his own tools; these consisted of very small floral forms of rather free treatment, and his decorative expression often consisted of the repetition of these tools in border form, or radiating corners. The background, being formed with dots and circles, gave a charming and refined texture to the decorated surface.

Since the days of Roger Payne, although England has stood high for technical merit in its bookbinding, it has lacked inventiveness in design until the arrival of Cobden Sanderson, since when all kinds of decorative expressions have been introduced, of which posterity, with its unprejudiced perspective view will be the best judge.

## CHAPTER XII

### FINISHING: (II) BOOK DECORATION

THE theory of practical book decoration, known technically as "finishing," is quite simple; in practice it is quite the reverse. The successful and necessarily expeditious handling of the tools to produce satisfactory results, can be acquired only after much practice, patient perseverance, and training. The accurate stamping of a tool with correct heat and with true register, the ability to run a fillet straight or a roll evenly, the mitring of the panel lines on the round of the back, and the true alignment of the lettering, whether it be type or hand-lettering, are features of prime importance not easily achieved.

Each leather and material requires its own special treatment in the preparation for gold tooling, and very often individual colours of leather require a difference in the heat necessary for perfect gilding. To begin with Levant morocco, which is perhaps considered as the first and foremost leather in use for fine bindings, the finisher receives the book already covered, and it may be necessary for him to moisten the cover with clean water, and roll the grain down. A smooth barrel-shaped roller, preferably of hard wood, is the best for this purpose. The amount of rolling must be determined by the size of the book, and the weight and hardness of the grain of the individual skin or part of the skin. Large books look better with a bold grain only slightly crushed, while small ones, especially if required for fine tooling, are better with the grain well crushed down. Some skins are very much harder than others, and an appreciable difference is to be found in different parts of the same

FIFTEENTH TO SIXTEENTH CENTURY

skin. The backbone and neck of Levant morocco are considerably harder than the flanks; and so, much judgment is necessary in exercising pressure on the roller, to equalize these variations.

When nearly dry, the book is marked up according to the decoration required. A very large majority of hand-tooled bindings are either framed in panel lines or composed of panel lines only. For the side these are usually marked direct on the leather, first with the compasses for position, then with a fine-pointed folder and straight-edge. For the back, lines are worked round the panels made by the bands. As a matter of convenience, the lines across the back are set just a fraction away from the bands, and the lines along the joint are set clear of the opening of the joint. Pallets (made of brass as are most finisher's tools) are tools with lines cut on their surface, and vary in length from $\frac{1}{8}$ in. to 3 in. The long pieces are used for impressing the lines across the back, the shorter ones up the back, and the pieces are selected according to the space between the bands. The head and tail panels are divided up like the remaining panels, and the spaces left beyond may be filled in with just a single line across at extreme head and tail, or a small panel may be added. Fillets, which are wheels with a line, or lines cut on their edges, are used for flat surfaces.

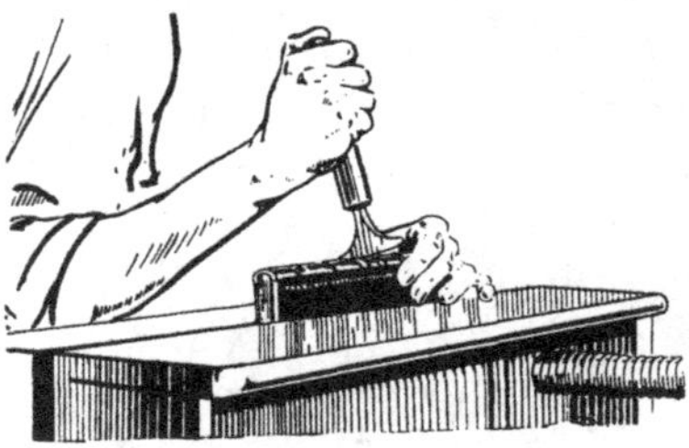

WORKING A PALLET

If the book is to be single-line panel only, then the marking up of the line round the side, and the line round each space between the bands, as well as at head and tail, is all that is necessary before putting on the preparations for the subsequent gilding. If there are more lines than one, the repetition of the first is all that is necessary, according to the number and proportionate width.

For convenience and expedition, the finisher will have pallets and fillets with two, three, or more lines cut on the surface; and varying widths and weight of line are stocked, so that a multiple-line panel up to a degree may be put on with almost as much ease as a single line, and with little additional cost beyond the mitring. The ends of the pallets are cut at an angle of 45°, so that a true mitre is obtained at each corner; and the fillet may have a piece cut out at a similar angle, so that the impressions may start true at the corner, and finish the same way at the end of the line; or the impressions may start away from the mitre, and the line be completed with the short pallet. When impressions are made on the leather before gilding, this process is referred to as "blind tooling." Simple designs may be worked direct on to the leather with the tools with perhaps one or two points as guidance for accuracy in placing; but elaborate and intricate patterns are blinded in through paper. The design is first made on a thin tough paper, preferably the thinnest Whatman

WORKING A FILLET

bank note, which is fixed on the book temporarily with a little tip of paste judiciously placed so as not to mark the leather. The tools, slightly heated, are then impressed into the leather through this paper. Fillets should never be impressed through paper, as the paper buckles in front of the running fillet and throws it all awry. The beginnings and ends only of straight lines are marked, and the impressions continued after the removal of the paper. Curved lines are made with gouges similar to the wood carver's chisel, blunted to the desired thickness. Gouges, being segments of circles, require to be changed every time the curve changes. Theoretically all curves are not segments of circles; but the skilled finisher can so manipulate his impressions as to follow almost any curve, perhaps not with the freedom and accuracy of a freehand drawn line, but tolerably correctly. One of the most difficult lines to follow is the true ellipse, as no part of its curve contains the segment of a circle.

WORKING A ROLL

To the uninitiated it would appear that with straight and curved lines the finisher should require nothing further in the way of tools, as those should compose all he requires. It has been the custom right from earliest times to have tools composed of complete units of ornamental forms engraved on the surface, and by repetition, alternation, and blending of units make up the required designs. The roll, which is a wheel with a complete design engraved on its edge, was amongst the earliest form of tool used; and much as it is despised

SIXTEENTH CENTURY (GROLIER)

by some people, it is still in constant demand commercially, and may even be used with true artistic effect.

The question of design in book decoration, as in all applied art, is an inexhaustible subject, and at this juncture one that must be left to individual taste and judgment.

When the design has been blinded in and the paper removed, inlays are then considered, if they are required. In Germany some very beautiful examples of inlaid work are to be seen, the full thickness of the leather being actually inlaid ; but in France and England this is rarely practised, as the nature of leather makes it prone to shrinkage, and, in consequence, the method is not acceptable. In the majority of cases, so-called " inlays " are not inlays at all, but merely thin leather stuck on the surface and well pressed in. In some cases the surface of the leather is removed and a corresponding thickness of surface leather substituted. This appears to be the most thorough method, as the two rough surfaces, stuck together and well pressed in, make for permanency and complete adhesion, with no danger of shrinkage. For repeating tools it is a matter of economy to have a corresponding punch to cut the inlays with, the best surface to cut on being lead. When the inlays are on, it is generally necessary to make the blind impression round them again thoroughly to set the edges. When all the blinding-in is done, the surface of the leather is washed with vinegar, not only to cleanse it, but to clear away any surface grease, and enable the subsequent preparations to sink in.

When this is partly dry, the impressions are pencilled in with glaire. Glaire consists of the white of eggs. One or two drops of vinegar are added to each white, then well beaten up and allowed to stand overnight, when it is ready for use. Albumen may be bought in

SIXTEENTH CENTURY (GROLIER)

dry crystals, to which water is added ; and when completely absorbed, it is strained off. This answers the purpose quite well, and is less troublesome to prepare. After the first coat of glaire has been pencilled in and allowed to dry, a second coating is applied, and when this is dry the book will be ready for laying on the gold. Although each successive preparation is allowed to dry it is only surface drying, and there should be sufficient moisture underneath for successful tooling. A fine sensitiveness to the heat of the tools used, and correct estimate of the amount of moisture under the surface of the leather, are the main secret of success in bright, clear, clean tooling.

The gold is laid out on the gold cushion and cut to size. The gold cushion is a padded board covered with a piece of good calf, the rough side being uppermost and smoothed down with bath brick. A little vaseline is taken up on a pad of cotton wool and rubbed over the prepared surface of the book, getting the vaseline well to the bottom of the impressions but not filling them. The gold is then picked up on a clean pad of cotton wool, laid over the greased surface, and pressed into the impressions. Two, three, or even more layers of gold may be necessary before all the breaks in the gold are covered. The laying-on pad should be firm and smooth to avoid breaking the gold, and by touching it on the face sufficient grease will be picked up to enable the gold to cling to the pad, when the well-greased surface of the leather will take it off again. No more should be prepared and laid on than can be worked off within a few hours.

White vaseline is best for delicate colours. Other forms of grease may be used, but should not be sufficiently penetrating to stain the leather. The tools are again worked into the impressions already made. The

SIXTEENTH CENTURY

heat of the tools is determined by laying the side of the tool on a pad of cotton wool saturated with water, lying in a saucer. When the tool ceases hissing and the moisture dries off quickly, it may be said to be ready to make the impression on the gold. There are so many varying factors at work that it is impossible to standardize the heat required. In fact, different finishers work with different temperatures on the same work, the difference in touch giving the same final results. When all the impressions have been made, the gold is cleaned off with a bit of soft rubber, then the grease is cleaned off with a pad of cotton wool saturated with benzoline. The soft rubber is made from pure rubber soaked in paraffin until it has the consistency of putty. This rubber will take up the gold and the refiner can reclaim it. Some finishers claim to get back almost 25 per cent of their outlay in gold leaf from their rubbers. Discrepancies in the amount of returns are very pronounced, and, whether it is the refiner or the finisher or the character of the work that makes the difference, it is impossible to determine. Some finishers use a soft rag saturated with oil in preference to rubber. Any portion of the tooling that is not perfect will have to be treated throughout as before.

COOLING A TOOL

The lettering on the back requires separate consideration. While it can be blinded in, in the same way as the rest of the tooling, most finishers prefer to work direct through the gold; maintaining that greater accuracy can be attained by this method. The lettering may be done in single letters, or set up in type. The surface is glaired all over and the gold laid on and a piece of cotton drawn across making a mark representing either the top of the line or the bottom, according to the preference of the finisher, or the nature of his type. For hand letters, the position of each letter is ticked off on the opposite side of the line to the one worked on, and the letters are worked off direct, with due calculation for thick and thin letters within the line, the main discrepancies being between letters I, M, and W.

In the case of type, the position of the first and last letter is found, due consideration being given to the round of the back, and the depth of the impression. The type is worked off in the same way as a pallet across the back. The gold is cleaned off, and, in the best work, the glaire is washed off and the impression worked in again. Glaire left on the surface of a book has a tendency to turn up white in the course of time unless varnished over, and no one really likes to varnish the surface of a Levant book, because the polished surface is in itself so rich, and not improved by the addition of varnish.

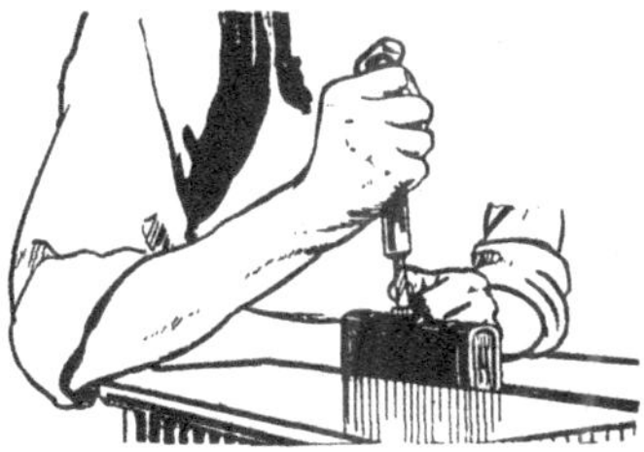

STRIKING A CENTRE TOOL

When all has been cleaned off and the effects of the benzoline allowed to evaporate, the book is ready for polishing. The iron used for the side is slightly barrel shaped, and the one on the back is flat across, but lengthwise it is more the segment of a circle, to get in between the bands. The heat used at first is very slight and the motion elliptical, never allowing the iron to rest for the fraction of a second. The surface of the iron is very smooth, bright, and clean. Every successive time the surface is polished over, the heat should be intensified and the pressure increased, until the desired polish is obtained. The whole book is then pressed between nickel or japanned plates and should remain at least twelve hours under moderate pressure.

Most moroccos may be treated in much the same manner as levant, with the chief exception that unlike levant they rarely require rolling while the surface is damp. Modern straight-grained and cross-grained moroccos are somewhat different, and so require some modification in finishing. There is already a prepared surface on these leathers which, if undisturbed in covering and kept quite clean, requires nothing but the glaire for making the gold adhere, and a very slight layer of varnish over the whole surface afterwards. This varnishing without previous preparation must not be undertaken without complete confidence in the leather and the covering. Any disturbance of the surface will cause the varnish to run in, and make very unsightly stains. A precautionary wash over with paste water will obviate this, but the final varnished surface will lose some of the bloom on which this leather relies for its chief charm.

Calf is perhaps the next in order of popularity for bookbindings, and requires entirely different treatment from morocco. Whatever is necessary in the way of gilt decoration is marked up first. No blinding-in is done in a general way, except the marking of the lines, and a few dot points to work to. If the pattern is of such a character that some blinding-in is necessary, this must be only of the very lightest touch. The calf is washed over with paste water, and allowed thoroughly to dry, when a coating of size follows. Vellum size and gelatine are both good. The paste water is just a

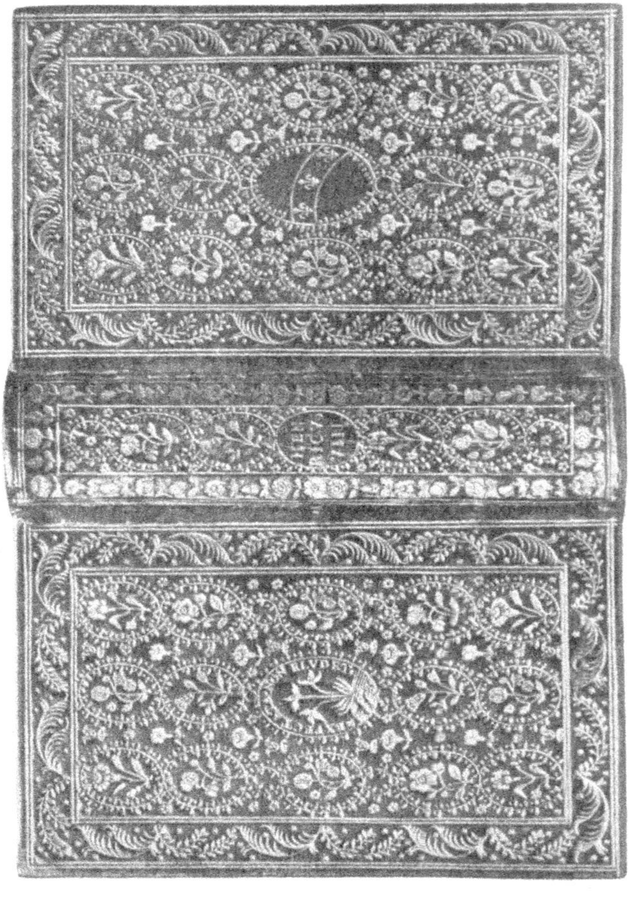

FRENCH SIXTEENTH TO SEVENTEENTH CENTURY (EVE)

mixture of flour paste and water to the consistency of good cream. The surface is glaired all over with a fine sponge. To minimize the glaire frothing when used with a sponge, a few drops of milk should be added to it. When the surface is dry, a second coating of glaire may be necessary, and, when that is dry, the gold is laid on, and the tools worked off. The heat required for tooling this leather is substantially in excess of that required for morocco. When the gold is cleaned off, the surface is varnished very slightly with a fine clear, quick-drying varnish. Extreme care must be taken in the handling of a calf book after the preparation has been put on, as the slightest bruise or scratch will allow the varnish to penetrate the leather, with dire consequences to its appearance. When quite dry, the book is pressed between polished plates.

Some finishers prefer to use starch for their first preparation in place of the paste water and size. This gives excellent results. The polishing iron is seldom used on calf, but, if it is necessary to get a very high polish on the surface, the iron is used, but with extreme care not to disturb the prepared surface. The surface of pigskin varies so much with different manufacturers that it is impossible to give any definite guide for its preparation for finishing. A very slight wash with very thin paste water before applying the glaire is generally adequate, and it is never improved by varnish.

Sheepskins are even more varied in their nature, and must be treated according to their individual characteristics, and the required effect after finishing. As a rule, these leathers may be treated in a similar manner to calf; and sealskin to moroccos. Vellum may be washed over with clean water, and then a mixture of sal-ammoniac and glaire, or the glaire may be carefully pencilled out into the impressions. Cloth and buckram

ENGLISH EIGHTEENTH CENTURY
(ROGER PAYNE)

usually require just a wash over with thin glaire ; but some of the coarser grained materials work better with a preliminary wash of paste water. Some silks can be worked with glaire pencilled in the impressions, but require excessively heated tools in finishing. A dry preparation is frequently used for silk, and always for velvet. This dry preparation, made from resinous substances reduced to the finest powder, is lightly dusted over the impressions, the gold being picked up on the tool, and worked off rather cool. This is known as " blocking powder," and is more in demand for edition work than for hand work. The finisher resorts to the use of blocking powder only under exceptional circumstances, but finds it extremely useful to him when he does. Most of the leather cloths that have been produced of recent years have been a veritable nightmare to the finisher. Some have achieved a fair measure of success with a prior use of methylated spirits, others appear to have discovered some preparation that they like to keep to themselves, or possibly their success may be in the individual touch or manipulation of the tool. Dry powder is generally successful, but not always a practical proposition.

So far hand finishing only has been considered, but it has been considered in most of its essential details, mainly because it must always be the fundamental principle on which developments are made for the large edition work, produced in the mass by the most up-to-date methods. The decoration on the machine-produced covers, whether of leather or cloth, is on precisely the same principle as the hand finishing, with certain modifications. Instead of stamping separate tools, an engraved or process block is made, taking the whole of the cover, which is impressed in a blocking press. The " blocking press " is precisely the same kind of press

ENGLISH EIGHTEENTH CENTURY
(ROGER PAYNE)

that was used by the early printers, and the development of the more modern power press still retains its similarity to the printing presses used for small work. The press is generally heated with gas, and the block attached to a plate with glue. The heat and pressure can be modified to any degree. The most recent development in the direction of blocking presses is the automatic feeding of the prepared gold leaf across the block, until the whole process is simplified to almost the same degree as the self-inking of the printing machine but with the use of real gold leaf and the heated block. While the preparation of the material is pretty much the same as that used for hand tooling, there is a considerable modification necessary in degree. Lesser and weaker quantities are required because the mechanical impression is much firmer and more definite than the hand process; and again, the making of a case is less disturbing to the material than is the making of the covered book. Much of the leather and fabric prepared to-day for the use of the edition binder is prepared with the idea of minimizing, or entirely obliterating, the use of any preparation whatsoever.

*By courtesy of Messrs. Krause*

BLOCKING PRESS

The developments that have taken place in the mass production of bookbinding within the last century are wonderful. It has only just turned the century since Archibald Leighton first used a material prepared by himself which was similar in character to much of the bookbinder's cloth in use to-day. Then the binder was a great craftsman, and the newly-fledged edition worker considered almost as inferior as his own cased

OMAR KHAYYAM

A SCHEME OF DECORATION CARRIED OUT IN GREEN INLAYS ON BLUE GROUND WITH SPOTS OF RED AND TOOLED IN BLIND AND GOLD

Designed and Executed by the Author

work in comparison with the aristocratic in-board worker.

Development and progress march onward, and to-day the edition worker is producing books almost as soundly

*By courtesy of The T. W. & C. B. Sheridan Co., Ltd.*

PRESS FOR STAMPING BOOK COVERS

constructed, and frequently more artistic than his aristocratic fellow craftsman, at a price which makes hand work look ridiculous. The skill of the hand worker is less appreciated and less in request, as the machine worker improves and creates a greater demand, and it is only a matter of conjecture as to how soon the in-board worker will be elbowed into a corner and forgotten by all but the real bibliophile.

Quite recently, one very large employer engaged in mass production expressed his preference for young men who had been trained in hand work, either at the technical schools or in workshops, because a workman so trained understood the working of his machines better than the workman not so trained. In short, he was still a craftsman, but the tools he used were machines driven by mechanical power. It therefore behoves us as craftsmen desiring progress and development, to keep in close touch with past methods of the old craftsmen of bygone days, for in their work are to be found the soundest principles of construction.

# APPENDIX

## THE FIRE HAZARDS OF PRINTING AND BOOKBINDING WORKS

By ROBERT TAYLOR, F.C.I.I.

IN a classification of printing and bookbinding works from the point of view of Fire Insurance, the undernoted would be included—

(*a*) General letter-press printing.

(*b*) Newspaper and magazine printing.

(*c*) Copper plate printing.

(*d*) Lithographic printing.

(*e*) Colour printing, not from type.

(*f*) Stereotyping and electrotyping.

(*g*) Bookbinding.

(*h*) Paper bag making, envelope making and cardboard box making.

(*i*) Stationery manufacture.

A perusal of a trade directory, or of one of the journals of the printing trade, will indicate what combinations of the above-named classes of work may be found in an individual risk.

The technique of bookbinding is dealt with in the foregoing pages. In the space available, it is impossible to give a similar outline of the technique of printing and other allied trades. For the purposes of this appendix, all that is necessary—so far as the main processes to be found in printing and bookbinding works are concerned—may be considered to be enumerated in a rough and ready fashion in the list set out above, and will be elaborated as may be necessary as the hazards arising from these and other ancillary processes are discussed.

The fire hazards of printing and bookbinding works may be set out in five main groups—

1. Hazards of the structure; possible defective construction; height; floor openings (hoists, stairs, wells, trap doors and the like); linings to walls and ceilings; partitions; situation (including exposure from other risks, or isolation necessitating adequate fire appliances).

2. Hazards of lighting, heating, and power (including boilers, engines, dynamos, motors, gas plants, and the like), also drying and the heating of materials.

3. Hazards of size or complexity (including cubical capacity or hands, or number or variety of machines, and plural tenure).

4. Hazards of materials—in use or applied (including risk of spontaneous combustion and non-removal of waste).

5. Hazards of management (including night work).

The fire hazard of any individual risk is not simply the addition of any of the hazards set out in the foregoing groups, but is determined by a consideration of the interplay of one group of hazards on another.

This interplay of hazard is of especial importance in printing and bookbinding risks, because so often—especially in smaller risks—buildings are old and or unsuitable for the purpose.

Mr. H. Cooke, in a paper read before the Insurance Institute of Yorkshire in 1904, gives an example of such a risk which is described as a " business, commenced in a dwelling-house, extended to a front shop, simply piled to the ceilings with stock, barely room for the eight or nine workpeople, which included the proprietor and his wife, to get round the machines and gas engine driving them."

But the old does not always mean the unsuitable from the point of view of the printer. I can recall a risk in what had been a fine, old dwelling-house, with a compositors' room on the attic floor, so perfect in its atmosphere as to recall the famous Plantin Museum of Antwerp, generally acknowledged to be one of the most interesting examples of an early printing works. The compositors' room, however, is probably the most innocuous part of a printers' premises, and this particular building was vitiated by the narrow wooden stairways from floor to floor, particularly that giving access to this compositors' room, and by the doubtful strength of the floors of the composing room. Where a composing room is of any size, there is considerable weight in the type metal contained in the room, and it is important that the walls and joists or girders supporting the floor should be strong enough to carry this weight. If in a composing room on the upper floor of a printing works there are also machines of the linotype class, this question of the weight-carrying capacity of the floor is still more apparent. A linotype machine weighs about a ton, and manufacturers recommend that floors where these machines are placed should be so constructed as to carry three hundredweights to the square foot.

It will be observed that in the preceding paragraph hazards of the first and third main groups of hazards set out above are illustrated, and before passing on to a consideration in greater detail of hazards of the other groups named, emphasis may again be laid on the necessity in the case of a printing and bookbinding works of not simply adding the various hazards of a particular risk, but of weighing them up in their relation one to another, so as to determine the hazard of that particular risk as a whole.

## Hazards of Lighting, Heating, and Power (Including Drying and the Heating of Materials)

**Lighting.** Lighting by electricity is to be preferred to lighting by coal gas. If the latter is used, there is danger in the use of naked jets near timber linings or partitions, or combustible goods or materials, and wooden ceilings over or near gas jets should be protected. Incandescent mantles require to be watched, as they have been the cause of fires through breaking when in use and falling on combustible goods or materials. Swinging brackets should be made more or less rigid, and fitted with globes or wire cages, as their proximity to the machines—particularly of the type of the usual wooden ruling machine to be found in bookbinding works—is a source of danger. In lighting up, a taper is to be preferred to matches, but most of all an electric lighter is to be preferred. If electric light is used, the installation should be in accordance with the regulations of the Institution of Electrical Engineers, or other recognized authority. Arc lamps should be of the approved type, so that there may be no risk of burning carbons falling on combustible goods or materials. Mr. Cooke, in his paper already referred to, illustrates the danger from unenclosed arc lights. He says—

" I remember one large works in Yorkshire where, on a certain Monday morning, a hole was found burned in the middle of a stack of printed sheets of a large size to a depth of one-and-a-half inches, and the only clue obtainable as to its cause was the suggestion of an electrician, that a hot carbon chip from the unenclosed arc light just overhead had dropped just before or as the lights were being switched off on the Saturday; and no doubt it was only the comparatively non-inflammable nature of paper when in close, solid contact (as was the case in question), which saved the premises from a serious and perhaps unaccountable fire."

**Heating.** Slow combustion stoves and gas radiators are the usual forms of heating in risks of this class, but systems of hot air, low pressure hot water, high or low pressure steam are not unusual. Stoves should stand on a fireproof base, a stone slab or bricks being most suitable, and the smoke pipe, if not of wrought iron, should be of substantial construction, and care should be taken that it is not within 9 in. of any combustible material, and that when passing close to, or through, partitions or roofs or other combustible material, it is enclosed in an earthenware collar, or asbestos protection provided. An adequate ash-pan is essential, and a stove standing on sheet iron on a wood floor is to be condemned. Where heating is by hot water or by high or low pressure steam, the pipes are better kept clear of wood or other combustible material. If they are rusty and there is any charring of the woodwork, oxidization occurs, setting up conditions favourable to a fire. Where hot air is in use, from a system in which heat radiates from the fire with surrounding ducts, sparks may be conveyed with the hot air if there is defective separation between fire and duct.

**Power.** Steam, gas, and electricity are commonly used. If electrical power is used, the installation—as in the case of a lighting installation—should be in accordance with the regulations of the Institution of Electrical Engineers or other recognized authority, motors, where not in separate compartments, being enclosed or thoroughly protected, and with other parts of the installation so placed as to be well clear of combustible materials. If steam power is used, the boiler should be in a separate compartment, preferably composition covered, and with adequate distance from the crown of the boiler to any non-fireproof floor or roof overhead. The necessity of keeping steam pipes clear of wood or other combustible material has already been mentioned in connection with heating. Gas engines should have exhaust pipe and box free from combustible material, and the bag protected by metal and not fixed against unprotected wood or subject to the chafing of a brick wall. Mr. Cameron, in the paper referred to later, emphasizes this risk from the exhaust pipe of a gas engine by citing an occasion when a surveyor, in the course of a survey, actually picked up an old sack in smouldering condition from an exhaust pipe partly embedded in a cement floor.

**Drying** of printed matter or of materials which have been varnished or gummed may be done, the printed sheets or varnished or gummed materials being suspended from lines or rods, or laid out on trays or racks. The heat employed may be derived from any of the methods of heating referred to under the items of " Heating " and " Power," and incidental fire hazards may be such as have already been mentioned under the items " Heating " and " Lighting." Separate drying rooms of fireproof construction are to be preferred. Where paper bags and envelopes are made by machinery, there is not the same necessity for laying out or hanging up to dry the gummed materials. In passing, it may be noted that the chief risk in envelope and paper bag making lies in the considerable quantity of loose paper exposed in the course of manufacture. There is present a distinct risk of fire in another method of drying, when printing is being done on both sides of a sheet of paper and the second printing is put in hand before the first has dried sufficiently. When one side of the sheet has been printed, some ink is apt to be left on the parchment of the tympan of the printing machine, and " sets-off " on the next sheet placed in the press. To avoid this, a thin sheet of paper, washed over with turpentine or saturated with benzine or oil, is pasted on the tympan. These "set-off" papers require to be changed from time to time, and should not be thrown down among other waste, but placed in a covered metal box and cleared daily.

**Heating of Materials.** The heating and melting of materials to be found in printing and bookbinding works may include the following—

(*a*) The melting of the composition which forms the coating of the inking rollers of a printing machine. This may be glue, treacle, and Paris white, or glue, glycerine and sugar, and a steam-heated pan should be employed for melting—not a large kettle over an open fire.

(*b*) Melting pots, gas-heated, are attached to linotype machines for the purpose of melting the type metal. The use of flexible, rubber piping for the gas burners is a hazard, because of the fraying of the rubber piping and the possible escape of gas.

(*c*) Gas is also freely used in stereotyping, though the melting pots for stereo work may be fuel heated. These melting pots should be set on a floor or base of fire-resisting construction, and rubber attachments to any gas stove should be avoided.

(*d*) In embossing, heat is employed in the preparation of the etched plate, which is fastened to its metal mount by pitch or by gutta percha dissolved in benzine or turpentine—sealing wax, indiarubber, or celluloid being sometimes used in the making of the counterparts. The risk of fire and explosion is thus considerable, celluloid or xylonite being inflammable explosive, and liable to spontaneous combustion. The risks of celluloid are well known, and have been the subject of official fire tests by the British Fire Prevention Committee, and were reported on by the Committee of five appointed by the Home Secretary some years ago, four of these being experts, one a principal Government chemist, one a Home Office Inspector of explosives, one Deputy Chief Inspector of Factories, and the fourth then Chairman of the British Fire Prevention Committee.

(*e*) Where bookbinding is done, gas rings are freely used on working benches for heating glue and for heating the finishing tools. They should be placed on metal trays and have metal collars, because of the litter on the benches. Gas-heated gold-blocking machines should have metal connections.

### Hazards of Materials in Use or Applied (Including Risk of Spontaneous Combustion, and Non-removal of Waste)

Some of the hazardous goods to be found in printing and bookbinding works have been mentioned in previous paragraphs. It only now remains to group the hazards from materials, which can best be done by indicating the purposes for which they are used, or the processes out of which the hazard arises.

The inks used by a printer are, as a rule, bought ready for use and thinned by boiled and raw linseed oils, or by vaseline, but a number of printers prepare their own ink, the materials used for the better qualities of black ink being lamp black and linseed oil, which by boiling at a high temperature becomes a colourless varnish; for cheaper kinds of ink a mineral oil product with rosin might be added to the lamp black. For colour work, the pigments employed for mixture with the varnish or other vehicle may be coal tar products or derived from mineral substances. Cleaning of the type in forme, or rollers, litho stones, etc., is done by benzine, paraffin, and turpentine.

Arrangements for the storage of these materials require attention, and if possible, only a supply of the oils or spirits in use sufficient for a day's needs should be brought into the main buildings. Lamp black, owing to its liability to spontaneous combustion, should be kept dry in metal vessels—its dust is explosive. All rags used in cleaning the type or machinery, owing to the risk of spontaneous combustion, should be kept in metal receptacles, and removed daily, or, if necessary, more than once a day. Where reams of paper are damped in troughs of water before printing, there is risk of spontaneous combustion arising from solid blocks of paper being stacked in a damp condition, but the practice is not so general as at one time. In newspaper printing, the damping done is by means of rollers forming part of the rotary machine, as the paper is supplied to the machine in reels.

### Hazards of Management (Including Night Work)

The acid test of the good management of printing and bookbinding works may be said to lie in the order and cleanliness displayed on the premises. There will be a willingness to comply with any reasonable suggestions for the reducing of any of the hazards set out above. Most of all, there will be appreciation that the litter of paper and other waste material, inevitable in risks of the class, should be cleared regularly and collected into bags or bins or tins, and removed at least once a week, oftener if possible. The state of the pits under the larger printing machines will furnish evidence as to the character of the management. This removal of paper and other waste is, if possible, more essential in the smaller risks referred to in the beginning of this appendix, and if in such a risk night work is necessary through spasmodic pressure of work, the hazard is increased, and may be greater still if smoking is carried on, whether by permission or surreptitiously.

Students of the subject may refer with advantage to the article appearing in Pitman's *Dictionary of Fire Insurance*, and to the paper by Mr. D. M. Cameron already mentioned, which appears in Volume VII of the *Journal of The Chartered Insurance Institute.* Anyone unfamiliar with the interior of a printing or bookbinding works will find the illustrations accompanying Mr. Cameron's paper helpful to an appreciation of some at least of the processes to be found in printing and bookbinding works.

# INDEX

PRINTED IN GREAT BRITAIN AT THE PITMAN PRESS, BATH
C—(1468J)

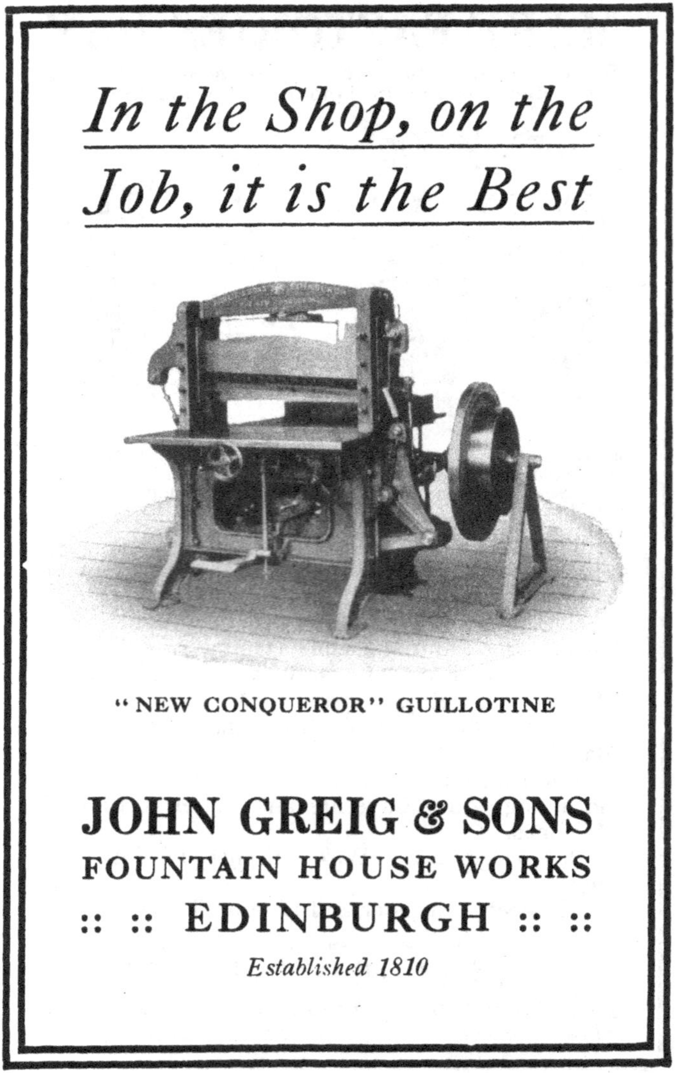

In the Shop, on the Job, it is the Best
"NEW CONQUEROR" GUILLOTINE
JOHN GREIG & SONS
FOUNTAIN HOUSE WORKS
:: :: EDINBURGH :: ::
Established 1810

A SELECTION FROM THE LIST OF

# COMMERCIAL HANDBOOKS

*PUBLISHED BY*

## SIR ISAAC PITMAN & SONS, LTD.

The following Catalogues will be sent post free on application: COMMERCIAL, EDUCATIONAL, TECHNICAL, SHORTHAND, FOREIGN LANGUAGES, and ART.

*Obtainable through any Bookseller or direct from the Publishers*

**LONDON: PARKER STREET, KINGSWAY, W.C.2**
**BATH: The Pitman Press. MELBOURNE: The Rialto, Collins Street.**
**NEW YORK: 2 West 45th Street. TORONTO: 70 Bond Street.**
**INDIA: A. H. Wheeler & Co., Hornby Road, Bombay; 11 Clive Street, Calcutta; and 15 Elgin Road, Allahabad.**

*The Prices contained in this List apply only to Great Britain.*

## CONTENTS

## ARITHMETIC, ETC.

PRICE

**Arithmetic and Book-keeping**
By Thos. Brown, F.S.S., and Vincent E. Collinge, A.C.I.S. In two parts. Part I . . . . . Net 2/6
Part II . . . . . . . . . . Net 1/3

**Arithmetic Class Book**
By W. R. Barham . . . . . . . . . 2/6

**Arithmetic Class Book**
**Advanced.** By W. R. Barham . . . . . 3/6

**Arithmetic of Commerce**
By P. W. Norris, M.A., B.Sc. (Hons.) . . Net 4/-

**Business Calculations**
By F. Heelis, F.C.I.S. . . . . . . . 2/-

**Commercial Invoicing**
By Max M. Kay . . . . . . . Net 1/6

**Commercial Mathematics**
By L. H. L. Davies, B.A., and E. G. H. Habakkuk . 5/-

**Complete Business Arithmetic** . . . . 4/-
**Answers** . . . . . . . . . Net 2/6

**Complete Mercantile Arithmetic**
By H. P. Green, F.C.Sp.T. (With Key) . Net 6/-

**Elements of Commercial Arithmetic**
By Thomas Brown . . . . . . Net 2/-

**Logarithms Simplified**
By Ernest Card, B.Sc., and A. C. Parkinson, A.C.P. . . . . . . . . . . Net 2/6

**Practical Commercial Arithmetic**
By H. Watson, B.Sc. (Econ.) . . . . . Net 6/-

**Principles and Practice of Commercial Arithmetic**
By P. W. Norris, M.A., B.Sc. . . . . Net 7/6

**Rapid Methods in Arithmetic**
By John Johnston. Revised and Edited by G. K. Bucknall, A.C.I.S. . . . . . . . Net 1/-

**Slide Rule Applied to Commercial Calculations, The** By R. M. Shireby . . . . Net 2/6

**Smaller Commercial Arithmetic**
By C. W. Crook, B.A., B.Sc. . . . . Net 2/-
**Answers** . . . . . . . . . Net 1/6

## BOOK-KEEPING AND ACCOUNTANCY

PRICE

**Accountants' Dictionary**
Edited by F. W. PIXLEY, F.C.A. In 2 Vols. . Net 67/6

**Accounting**
By S. S. DAWSON, M.Com., F.C.A., and R. C. DE ZOUCHE, F.C.A. . . . . . . . . . Net 10/6

**Accounts of Executors, Administrators, and Trustees**
By WILLIAM B. PHILLIPS, F.C.A., A.C.I.S. . Net 5/-

**Advanced Accounts**
Edited by ROGER N. CARTER, M.Com., F.C.A. . Net 7/6

**Key to Advanced Accounts**
By R. A. GOODMAN . . . . . . . 20/-

**Advanced Book-keeping Exercises for Commercial Schools**
By A. J. FAVELL, B.Sc.(Econ.), A.C.I.S. . . . 2/6

**Apportionment in Relation to Trust Accounts**
By A. F. CHICK, *Incorporated Accountant* . Net 6/-

**Auditing, Accounting, and Banking**
By F. DOWLER, A.C.A., and E. M. HARRIS, A.I.B. Net 7/6

**Auditors: Their Duties and Responsibilities**
By F. W. PIXLEY, F.C.A. . . . . . Net 21/-

**Audit Programmes**
By E. E. SPICER, F.C.A., and E. C. PEGLER, F.C.A. Net 4/6

**Balance Sheets, Business**
By F. R. STEAD . . . . . . . . Net 10/6

**Book-keeper's Vade Mecum, The**
By S. HOWARD WITHEY, F.C.I., A.L.A.A. . . Net 3/6

**Book-keeping, A Course in**
By R. W. HOLLAND, O.B.E., M.A., M.Sc., LL.D. Net 4/-

**Book-keeping and Accounts**
By E. E. SPICER, F.C.A., and E. C. PEGLER, F.C.A. Net 20/-

**Book-keeping and Office Work**
By R. J. PORTERS, F.C.R.A. Two Vols. . . Net 30/-

**Book-keeping for Beginners**
By W. E. HOOPER, A.C.I.S. . . . . . Net 2/-

## Book-keeping and Accountancy—contd.

PRICE

**Book-keeping for Retailers**
By H. W. Porritt and W. Nicklin, A.S.A.A. . Net 2/-

**Book-keeping for Shopkeepers**
By J. Greig, F.C.I. . . . .. . . Net 2/6

**Book-keeping, Modern Methods of**
By R. H. Epps, *Chartered Accountant* . . Net 4/-

**Branch Accounts**
By P. Taggart. A.S.A.A. . . . . . Net 3/-

**Builders' Accounts and Costs**
By Robert G. Legge . . . . . . Net 3/6

**Business Book-keeping**
By J. Routley . . . . . . . Net 3/6

**Club Accounts**
By C. A. Holliday, A.S.A.A. . . . . Net 3/6

**Commercial Goodwill**
By P. D. Leake, F.C.A. . . . . . Net 21/-

**Company Accounts**
By Arthur Coles. Revised by W. C. Wood, A.C.I.S. . . . . . . . . . Net 7/6

**Consignments, Account Sales, and Accounts Current**
By E. J. Hammond, A.C.I.S., A.L.A.A. . . Net 5/-

**Cost Accounting**
By W. B. Lawrence, C.P.A. . . . . . Net 21/-

**Cost Accounts in Principle and Practice**
By A. Clifford Ridgway, F.C.A. . . . Net 5/-

**Cost Accounts for the Metal Industry**
By H. E. Parkes, M.Com., A.C.W.A. . . Net 10/6

**Costing and Price Fixing**
By J. M. Scott Maxwell, B.Sc., F.C.W.A. . Net 6/-

**Costing, A Primer of**
By R. J. H. Ryall . . . . . . Net 5/-

**Costing, Dictionary of**
By R. J. H. Ryall . . . . . . Net 10/6

**Costing, Theory and Practice of**
By E. W. Newman, F.C.A. . . . . . Net 8/6

**Costs for Manufacturers**
By C. Smith . . . . . . . . Net 5/-

**Depreciation and Wasting Assets**
By P. D. Leake, F.C.A. . . . . . Net 15/-

**Dictionary of Book-keeping**
By R. J. Porters, F.C.R.A. . . . . . Net 7/6

| | | PRICE |
|---|---|---|
| **Estimating**<br>By T. H. Hargrave . . . . . . | Net | 7/6 |
| **Executorship Accounts**<br>By C. Townsend . . . . . . . | Net | 5/- |
| **Foreign Exchange Accounting**<br>By C. Djoröp . . . . . . . | Net | 15/- |
| **Full Course in Book-keeping**<br>By H. W. Porritt and W. Nicklin, A.S.A.A. | Net | 5/- |
| **Graded Book-keeping Exercises for Commercial Schools**<br>By A. J. Favell, B.Sc., A.C.I.S. . . . . . | | 2/- |
| **Higher Book-keeping and Accounts**<br>By H. W. Porritt and W. Nicklin, A.S.A.A. | Net | 5/- |
| **Holding Companies**<br>By A. J. Simons, A.C.A. (Hons.) . . . | Net | 10/6 |
| **Hotel Book-keeping** . . . . . . | Net | 2/6 |
| **Manual of Cost Accounts**<br>By H. Julius Lunt, F.C.A., F.C.I.S., F.C.W.A. | Net | 7/6 |
| **Notes of Lessons on Book-keeping**<br>By J. Routley . . . . . . . | Net | 3/6 |
| **Practical Auditing**<br>By E. E. Spicer, F.C.A., and E. C. Pegler, F.C.A. | Net | 21/- |
| **Principles of Accounts**<br>By J. Stephenson, M.A., M.Com., D.Sc.<br>Part I, 3/6 . . . . Part II | | 5/- |
| **Principles of Auditing**<br>By F. R. M. De Paula, O.B.E., F.C.A. . . | Net | 7/6 |
| **Principles of Book-keeping Explained**<br>By I. H. Humphrys . . . . . . . | Net | 2/6 |
| **Questions and Answers in Book-keeping and Accounting.** By F. F. Sharles, F.S.A.A. . | Net | 10/6 |
| **Railway Accounts**<br>By C. H. Newton, F.A.A. . . . . . | Net | 10/6 |
| **Sharles's Elementary Book-keeping**<br>By F. F. Sharles, F.S.A.A., F.C.I.S. . . . . | | 3/6 |
| **Shopkeepers' Accounts Simplified**<br>By C. D. Cornell . . . . . . . | Net | 2/- |
| **Sinking Funds, Reserve Funds, and Depreciation.** By J. H. Burton, A.S.A.A. . . | Net | 3/6 |

## CAREERS, ETC.

| | | PRICE |
|---|---|---|
| **Authorship and Journalism**<br>By ALBERT E. BULL | Net | 3/6 |
| **Banking as a Career**<br>By F. A. WILLMAN, Cert. A.I.B. | Net | 3/6 |
| **Game of Commerce, The**<br>By HERBERT KENDRICK | Net | 3/6 |
| **How to Become an Auctioneer and Estate Agent**<br>By W. F. NOKES, F.A.T. | Net | 3/6 |
| **How to Become a Company Secretary**<br>By E. J. HAMMOND, A.C.I.S. | Net | 3/6 |
| **How to Become a Private Secretary**<br>By J. E. MCLACHLAN, F.I.P.S. (Hons.) | Net | 3/6 |
| **How to Become a Qualified Accountant**<br>By R. A. WITTY, F.S.A.A. | Net | 3/6 |
| **How to Choose Your Career**<br>By W. LESLIE IVEY, M.C. | Net | 3/6 |
| **How to Secure a Good Job**<br>By W. LESLIE IVEY, M.C. | Net | 3/6 |
| **Journalism as a Career**<br>Edited by W. T. CRANFIELD | Net | 5/- |

## CIVIL SERVICE

| | | |
|---|---|---|
| **Civil Service Arithmetic Tests**<br>By P. J. VARLEY-TIPTON | Net | 2/6 |
| **Civil Service Essay Writing**<br>By W. J. ADDIS, M.A. | Net | 2/6 |
| **Civil Service Guide**<br>By A. J. LAWFORD JONES | Net | 2/6 |
| **Civil Service Practice in Précis Writing**<br>Edited by ARTHUR REYNOLDS, M.A. (Oxon) | Net | 2/6 |
| **Copying Manuscript, Orthography, Handwriting, etc.**<br>By A. J. LAWFORD JONES | Net | 3/6 |
| **Elementary Précis Writing**<br>By WALTER SHAWCROSS, B.A. | Net | 2/- |
| **Guide to Indexing and Précis Writing**<br>By W. J. WESTON, M.A., B.Sc., and E. BOWKER | Net | 2/- |

## COMMERCE, ETC.

| | | PRICE |
|---|---|---|
| **Commerce for Commercial and Secondary Schools**<br>By A. J. Favell, B.Sc.(Econ.), A.C.I.S. | | 3/6 |
| **Commerce, Stage I**<br>By A. James, F.F.T.Com., F.R.Econ.S. | | 2/6 |
| **Commercial Handwriting and Correspondence** | Net | 2/6 |
| **Commercial Practice**<br>By Alfred Schofield, B.Sc. (Econ.) | Net | 3/6 |
| **Elements of Commerce**<br>By F. Heywood, F.C.I.S. | Net | 4/- |
| **How to Study for Examinations**<br>By D. Cooper | | 2/- |
| **Manual of Business Training** | Net | 4/- |
| **Modern Business and Its Methods**<br>By W. Campbell, *Chartered Secretary* | Net | 7/6 |
| **Popular Guide to Journalism**<br>By A. Kingston | Net | 2/6 |
| **Practical Journalism and Newspaper Law**<br>By A. Baker, M.J.I., and E. A. Cope | Net | 3/6 |
| **Principles and Practice of Commerce**<br>By James Stephenson, M.A., M.Com., D.Sc. | Net | 8/6 |
| **Principles of Business**<br>By James Stephenson, M.A., M.Com., D.Sc.<br>Part I, Net **2/6**; Part II, | Net | 3/6 |
| **Questions and Answers on Commerce. Stage I**<br>By A. J. Favell, B.Sc. (Econ.), A.C.I.S. | Net | 2/6 |
| **Questions and Answers on Business Practice**<br>By E. J. Hammond, A.C.I.S., A.L.A.A. | Net | 5/- |
| **Routine of Commerce**<br>By Alfred Schofield, B.Sc.(Econ.) | Net | 4/- |
| **Short Story Writing and Free Lance Journalism**<br>By Sydney A. Moseley | Net | 7/6 |
| **Theory and Practice of Commerce**<br>Edited by F. Heelis, F.C.I.S. | Net | 7/6 |
| **Wholesale and Retail Trade**<br>By W. Campbell | Net | 5/- |

## ENGLISH AND COMMERCIAL CORRESPONDENCE

| | | PRICE |
|---|---|---|
| **Business Letters in English**<br>By W. J. WESTON, M.A., B.Sc. | Net | 3/6 |
| **Commerce and Correspondence**<br>By E. H. GROUT, B.Sc.(Econ.) | Net | 5/- |
| **Commercial Correspondence and Commercial English** | Net | 3/6 |
| **Commercial Dictionary** | Net | 1/6 |
| **Correspondence of Commerce, The**<br>By A. RISDON PALMER, B.Sc., B.A. | Net | 4/- |
| **Dictionary of Correct English, A**<br>By M. A. PINK, M.A. | Net | 2/6 |
| **English and Commercial Correspondence**<br>By H. NAGAOKA and D. THEOPHILUS, B.A. | | 3/6 |
| **English Composition and Business Correspondence**<br>By J. F. DAVIS, D.Lit., M.A., LL.B. (Lond.) | Net | 2/- |
| **English Exercises. A Book of Homonyms**<br>By B. S. BARRETT | | 3/6 |
| **English for Commercial Students**<br>By H. W. HOUGHTON | Net | 2/6 |
| **English Grammar and Composition**<br>By W. J. WESTON, M.A., B.Sc. (Lond.) | Net | 4/6 |
| **English Mercantile Correspondence** | Net | 3/6 |
| **Guide to Commercial Correspondence**<br>By W. J. WESTON, M.A., B.Sc. (Lond.) | | 2/6 |
| **How to Teach Commercial English**<br>By WALTER SHAWCROSS, B.A. | Net | 3/6 |
| **Manual of Commercial English**<br>By WALTER SHAWCROSS, B.A. | Net | 3/6 |
| **Manual of Punctuation.** By W. D. WEBSTER | | 1/- |
| **New Era Spelling Manual**<br>By H. J. BOWER | | 2/6 |
| **Pocket English Dictionary** | Net | 1/6 |
| **Principles and Practice of Commercial Correspondence.** By J. STEPHENSON, M.A., M.Com. | Net | 7/6 |
| **Punctuation as a Means of Expression**<br>By A. E. LOVELL, M.A. | Net | 1/- |
| **Synonyms and Antonyms, Pitman's Book of** | Net | 2/6 |

## GEOGRAPHY AND HISTORY

| | | PRICE |
|---|---|---|
| **Commercial Atlas of the World** . . | Net | 5/- |
| **Commercial Geography of the British Empire Abroad and Foreign Countries** . . | Net | 3/- |
| **Commercial Geography of the British Isles** . . . . . . . . | Net | 2/6 |
| **Commercial Geography of the World** . | Net | 4/6 |
| **Commercial History**<br>By J. R. V. MARCHANT, M.A. . . . . | Net | 5/6 |
| **Economic Geography**<br>By John MCFARLANE, M.A., M.Com. . . | Net | 10/6 |
| **Economic Geography, The Principles of**<br>By R. N. RUDMOSE BROWN . . . . . | Net | 6/- |
| **Economic Resources of the Empire**<br>Edited by T. WORSWICK, O.B.E., M.Sc. . . | Net | 5/- |
| **Elements of Commercial Geography**<br>By C. H. GRANT, M.Sc., F.R.Met.Soc. . . | Net | 2/- |
| **Elements of Commercial History**<br>By FRED HALL, M.A., B.Com., F.C.I.S. . . | Net | 2/- |
| **Geography of Commerce, The**<br>By W. P. RUTTER, M.Com. . . . . . | Net | 5/- |
| **History of Commerce, The**<br>By T. G. WILLIAMS, M.A., F.R.Hist.S., F.R.Econ.S. | Net | 5/- |
| **Main Currents of Social and Industrial Change, 1870-1924**<br>By T. G. WILLIAMS, M.A. . . . . . | Net | 5/- |
| **Outlines of the Economic History of England**<br>By H. O. MEREDITH, M.A., M.Com. . . . | Net | 7/6 |
| **Principles of Commercial History**<br>By J. STEPHENSON, M.A., M.Com., D.Sc. . | Net | 7/6 |
| **Rise of British Commerce, The**<br>By K. G. LEWIS, B.A., and N. BRANTON . . | | 3/6 |
| **Statistical Atlas of the World, A**<br>By J. STEPHENSON, M.A., M.Com., D.Sc. | Net | 7/6 |

## ECONOMICS

| | | PRICE |
|---|---|---|
| **Dictionary of Economic and Banking Terms**<br>By W. J. WESTON, M.A., B.Sc., and A. CREW . | Net | 5/- |
| **Economics Educator**<br>Edited by J. H. JONES, M.A. Three Vols. . | Net | 63/- |
| **Economics for Business Men**<br>By W. J. WESTON, M.A., B.Sc. . . . . | Net | 3/6 |
| **Economics for Everyman**<br>By J. E. LE ROSSIGNOL . . . . . | Net | 5/- |
| **Economics of Private Enterprise, The**<br>By J. H. JONES, M.A. . . . . . . | Net | 7/6 |
| **Economics of Instalment Trading and Hire Purchase.** By W. F. CRICK . . . . | Net | 5/- |
| **Economics of the Manufacturing Business**<br>By W. A. STEWART JONES, F.C.W.A., F.S.S. . . | | 3/6 |
| **Economics of the Wholesale and Retail Trade**<br>By JAMES STEPHENSON, M.A., M.COM., D.Sc. . . | | 5/- |
| **Elements of Political Economy**<br>By H. HALL, B.A. . . . . . . | Net | 2/- |
| **Exercises in Economics**<br>By A. PLUMMER, M.Sc. (Econ.), M.A., LL.D. . | Net | 2/- |
| **Guide to Political Economy**<br>By F. H. SPENCER, D.Sc., LL.B. . . . | Net | 3/6 |
| **Industrial Combination in England**<br>By P. FITZGERALD, D.Sc.(Econ.) . . . | Net | 10/6 |
| **Introduction to Business Economics**<br>By J. STEPHENSON, M.A., M.Com., D.Sc. . . | | 3/6 |
| **Outlines of Central Government**<br>By JOHN J. CLARKE, M.A., F.S.S. . . | Net | 5/- |
| **Outlines of Industrial and Social Economics**<br>By JOHN J. CLARKE, M.A., F.S.S., and JAMES E. PRATT, A.C.I.S. . . . . . . . . . . | Net | 1/6 |
| **Outlines of Local Government of the United Kingdom (and the Irish Free State)**<br>By JOHN J. CLARKE, M.A., F.S.S. . . . | Net | 5/- |
| **Plain Economics**<br>By JOHN LEE, M.A., M.Com.Sc. . . . . | Net | 3/6 |
| **Principles of Economics**<br>By L. A. RUFENER, Ph.D. . . . . . | Net | 16/- |
| **Substance of Economics, The**<br>By H. A. SILVERMAN, B.A. (Econ.) . . . | Net | 6/- |

## BANKING AND FINANCE

PRICE

**Answers to Questions Set at the Examinations of the Institute of Bankers**

By L. L. M. Minty, Ph.D., B.Sc., Econ., B.Com.—

| | | | |
|---|---|---|---|
| Foreign Exchange. Part I & Part II | Each | Net | 3/6 |
| Economics. Part I & Part II . . | Each | Net | 5/– |
| English Grammar and Composition. Part I | | Net | 3/6 |
| ,, ,, ,, ,, Part II . | | Net | 5/– |

**Banker as a Lender, The**

By F. E. Steele . . . . . . . Net 5/–

**Bankers' Advances**

By F. R. Stead. Edited by Sir John Paget, K.C. Net 6/–

**Bankers' Advances Against Produce**

By A. Williams, A.I.B. . . . . . Net 6/–

**Bankers and the Property Statutes of 1925 and 1926.** By R. W Jones . . . Net 6/–

**Bankers' Credits**

By W. F. Spalding . . . . . . Net 10/6

**Bankers' Securities Against Advances**

By Lawrence A. Fogg, Cert. A.I.B. . . Net 6/–

**Bankers' Clearing House, The**

By P. W. Matthews . . . . . . Net 7/6

**Bankers' Tests**

By F. R. Stead . . . . . . . Net 10/6

**Bank Organization, Management, etc.**

By J. F. Davis, M.A., D.Lit., LL.B. (Lond.) . Net 6/–

**Bills of Exchange Act, 1882, The**

By M. H. Megrah, B.Com. . . . . . Net 6/–

**Bills of Exchange Acts, A Practical Examination of the**

By C. H. Fennell . . . . . . Net 7/6

**Cheques.** By C. F. Hannaford . . . Net 6/–

**Dictionary of Banking**

By W. Thomson . . . . . . . Net 30/–

**Dictionary of Banking Terms in Three Languages, (English-French-German)**

By L. Herendi . . . . . . . Net 21/–

**Dictionary of the World's Currencies and Foreign Exchanges**

By W. F. Spalding . . . . . . Net 30/–

**Discount Market in London, The**

By H. W. Greengrass . . . . . Net 6/–

## Banking and Finance—contd.

PRICE

**Eastern Exchange, Currency, and Finance**
By W. F. Spalding . . . . . . . Net 15/-

**Elements of Banking**
By J. P. Gandy . . . . . . . Net 2/-

**English Banking Administration, An Outline of**
By Joseph Sykes, B.A. (Hons.) . . . . Net 2/6

**English Banking Methods**
By L. L. M. Minty, Ph.D., B.Sc., B.Com. . Net 15/-

**English Composition and Banking Correspondence**
By L. E. W. O. Fullbrook-Leggatt, M.C., B.A. Net 5/-

**Foreign Banking Systems**
By H. Parker Willis and B. H. Beckhart . Net 21/-

**Foreign Exchange and Foreign Bills in Theory and in Practice.** By W. F. Spalding . Net 7/6

**Foreign Exchange, A Primer of**
By W. F. Spalding . . . . . . . Net 3/6

**Foreign Exchanges, Arithmetic and Practice of the.** By A. G. Sugg, Cert. A.I.B. . . Net 3/6

**Foreign Trade, The Finance of**
By W. F. Spalding . . . . . . . Net 7/6

**Functions of Money, The**
By W. F. Spalding . . . . . . . Net 7/6

**London Money Market, The**
By W. F. Spalding . . . . . . . Net 10/6

**Money, Exchange, and Banking**
By H. T. Easton, A.I.B. . . . . . Net 6/-

**Notes on Banking and Commercial Law**
By T. Lloyd Davies . . . . . . Net 3/-

**Practical Banking**
By J. F. G. Bagshaw, Cert. A.I.B. . . . Net 7/6

**Theory and Principles of Central Banking, The**
By William A. Shaw, Litt.D. . . . . Net 12/6

**Theory and Practice of Finance, The**
By W. Collin Brooks . . . . . . . Net 10/6

**Title Deeds Old and New**
By Francis R. Stead. . . . . . Net 5/-

## INSURANCE

PRICE

**Actuarial Science, The Elements of**
By R. E. UNDERWOOD, M.B.E., F.I.A. . . . Net 5/-

**Average Clauses and Fire-Loss Apportionments.** By E. H. MINNION, F.C.I.I. . . . Net 8/6

**Building Construction, Plan Drawing, and Surveying in Relation to Fire Insurance**
By D. W. WOOD, M.B.E. . . . . . . Net 6/-

**Burglary Risks**
By E. H. GROUT, B.Sc., A.C.I.I. . . . . Net 10/6

**Business Man's Guide to Insurance, The**
By A. PHILPOTT . . . . . . . . Net 3/6

**Casualty Insurance**
By C. J. CROBAUGH, M.A., and A. E. REDDING, B.S. Net 25/-

**Compound Interest, Principles of**
By H. H. EDWARDS . . . . . . Net 5/-

**Dictionary of Accident Insurance**
Edited by J. B. WELSON, LL.M., F.C.I.I., F.C.I.S. Net 60/-

**Fire Extinguishment and Fire Alarm Systems**
By R. NORTHWOOD . . . . . . . Net 7/6

**Fire Insurance, Common Hazards of**
By W. G. KUBLER RIDLEY, F.C.I.I. . . . Net 5/-

**Fire Insurance, Dictionary of**
Edited by B. C. REMINGTON, F.C.I.I. . . . Net 30/-

**Fire Insurance, Principles and Practice of**
By F. GODWIN . . . . . . . . Net 5/-

**Fire Insurance, The Law of**
By J. ROWLATT, B.A. . . . . . . . Net 7/6

**Fire Policy Drafting and Endorsements**
By W. C. H. DARLEY . . . . . . . Net 7/9

**Fire Waste.** By G. E. KEAY . . . . . Net 2/6

**Guide to Marine Insurance**
By HENRY KEATE . . . . . . . . Net 3/6

**Insurance**
By T. E. YOUNG, B.A., F.I.A., F.R.A.S. . . . Net 10/6

**Insurance Office Organization and Routine**
By J. B. WELSON, LL.M., F.C.I.I., F.C.I.S., and F. H. SHERRIFF, F.I.A. . . . . . . . . Net 7/6

**Insurance of Profits.** By A. G. MACKEN . Net 5/-

**Insurance of Public Liability Risks**
By S. V. KIRKPATRICK, F.C.I.I. . . . . Net 5/-

## Insurance—contd.

PRICE

**Law and Practice as to Fidelity Guarantees**
By C. EVANS and F. H. JONES . . . . Net 6/-

**Law of Accident and Contingency Insurance**
By F. H. JONES . . . . . . . . Net 7/6

**Law of Negligence**
By J. B. WELSON, LL.M., F.C.I.I., F.C.I.S. . Net 5/-

**Life Assurance from Proposal to Policy**
By H. HOSKING TAYLOR, F.I.A., A.C.I.I., and V. W. TYLER, F.I.A. . . . . . . . Net 6/-

**Life Assurance, Dictionary of**
Edited by G. W. RICHMOND, F.I.A., and F. H. SHERRIFF, F.I.A. . . . . . . . . . . Net 50/-

**Life Assurance, Guide to**
By S. G. LEIGH, F.I.A. . . . . . . Net 5/-

**Marine Insurance of Goods, The**
By F. W. S. POOLE . . . . . . Net 15/-

**Motor Insurance.** By W. F. TODD . . Net 6/-

**Pension and Superannuation Funds, Their Formation and Administration Explained**
By BERNARD ROBERTSON, F.I.A., and H. SAMUELS Net 5/-

**Pension, Endowment, Life Assurance, and Other Schemes for Commercial Companies**
By H. DOUGHARTY, F.C.I.I. . . . . . Net 6/-

**Personal Accident, Disease, and Sickness Insurance, The Principles and Practice of**
By J. B. WELSON, LL.M. . . . . . Net 5/-

**Physiology and Anatomy**
By H. GARDINER, M.S., F.R.C.S. . . . . Net 10/6

**Principles and Practice of Accident Insurance**
By G. E. BANFIELD, A.C.I.I. . . . . . Net 6/-

**Principles of Insurance.** By J. ALFRED EKE Net 5/-

**Successful Insurance Agent, The**
By J. J. BISGOOD, B.A., F.C.I.S., J.P. . . . Net 2/6

**Talks on Insurance Law**
By J. A. WATSON, B.Sc., LL.B. . . . . Net 3/6

**Workmen's Compensation Insurance**
By C. E. GOLDING, LL.D., F.C.I.I., F.S.S. . Net 5/-

## SHIPPING

| | | PRICE |
|---|---|---|
| **Case and Freight Costs** By A. W. E. CROSFIELD | Net | 2/- |
| **Exporters' Handbook and Glossary, The** By F. M. DUDENEY | Net | 7/6 |
| **How to Export Goods.** By F. M. DUDENEY | Net | 2/- |
| **How to Import Goods.** By J. A. DUNNAGE | Net | 2/- |
| **Import and Export Trade.** By A. S. HARVEY | Net | 21/- |
| **Importer's Handbook, The.** By J. A. DUNNAGE | Net | 10/6 |
| **Manual of Exporting** By J. A. DUNNAGE, F.S.S., F.C.I., A.M.Inst.T. | Net | 10/6 |
| **Shipbroking, Introduction to** By C. D. MACMURRAY and M. M. CREE | Net | 3/6 |
| **Shipping.** By A. HALL and F. HEYWOOD | Net | 2/- |
| **Shipping and Shipbroking** By C. D. MACMURRAY and M. M. CREE | Net | 15/- |
| **Shipping Business Methods** By R. B. PAUL | Net | 5/- |
| **Shipping Finance and Accounts** By R. B. PAUL | Net | 2/6 |
| **Shipping Office Organization, Management, and Accounts.** By ALFRED CALVERT | Net | 6/- |
| **Shipping Terms and Phrases** By J. A. DUNNAGE | Net | 2/6 |

## INCOME TAX

| | | |
|---|---|---|
| **Income Tax, Introduction to** By E. D. FRYER, A.L.A.A. | Net | 2/6 |
| **Income Tax, Notes on** By W. S. CARRINGTON, *Chartered Accountant* | Net | 3/6 |
| **Income Tax, Snelling's Practical** By C. W. CHIVERS | Net | 3/6 |
| **Income Tax Relief, Double** By H. E. SEED and A. W. RAWLINSON | Net | 10/6 |
| **Income Tax Reliefs** By A. W. RAWLINSON, A.C.A. | Net | 20/- |
| **Income Tax, Super-Tax, and Surtax** **The New Law Explained** By V. WALTON, F.C.A., F.R.S., F.R.Econ.S. | Net | 7/6 |

## SECRETARIAL WORK, ETC.

| | | PRICE |
|---|---|---|
| **Chairman's Manual** | | |
| By Gurdon Palin, and Ernest Martin, F.C.I.S. | Net | 5/- |
| **Company Registrar's Manual, The** | | |
| By J. J. Quinlivan . . . . . . | Net | 10/6 |
| **Company Secretarial Work** | | |
| By E. Martin, F.C.I.S. . . . . . . | Net | 2/- |
| **Company Secretary's Vade Mecum** | | |
| Edited by P. Tovey, F.C.I.S. Revised by C. W. Adams, A.C.I.S. . . . . . . . . | Net | 3/6 |
| **Dictionary of Secretarial Law and Practice** | | |
| Edited by Philip Tovey, F.C.I.S. . . . . | Net | 50/- |
| **Examination Notes on Secretarial Practice** | | |
| By C. W. Adams, A.C.I.S. . . . . . | Net | 2/6 |
| **Formation and Management of a Private Company** | | |
| By F. D. Head, B.A. . . . . . . | Net | 7/6 |
| **Guide for the Company Secretary** | | |
| By Arthur Coles. Revised by W. Cecil Wood, A.C.I.S. . . . . . . . . . | Net | 6/- |
| **Guide to Company Secretarial Work** | | |
| By O. Oldham, A.C.I.S. Revised by G. K. Bucknell, A.C.I.S. (Hons.) . . . . . . . | Net | 3/6 |
| **Honorary Secretaryship** | | |
| By W. B. Thorne . . . . . . | Net | 2/6 |
| **How to Take Minutes** | | |
| Edited by E. Martin, F.C.I.S. . . . . | Net | 2/6 |
| **Meetings** | | |
| By F. D. Head, B.A. . . . . . . | Net | 5/- |
| **Outlines of Transfer Procedure in Connection with Stocks, Shares, etc.** | | |
| By F. D. Head, B.A. (Oxon), *Barrister-at-Law* . | Net | 3/6 |
| **Practical Secretarial Work** | | |
| By Henry I. Lee, A.I.S.A., *Incorporated Secretary*, and William N. Barr . . . . . . | Net | 7/6 |
| **Practical Share Transfer Work** | | |
| By F. W. Liddington . . . . . . | Net | 3/6 |
| **Questions and Answers on Secretarial Practice** | | |
| By E. J. Hammond. Revised by G. K. Bucknall, A.C.I.S. (Hons.) . . . . . . . | Net | 7/6 |
| **Secretary's Handbook** | | |
| Edited by Sir H. E. Blain, C.B.E. . . . | Net | 5/- |
| **Transfer of Stocks, Shares, and Other Marketable Securities** | | |
| By F. D. Head, B.A. . . . . . . | Net | 7/6 |

## INDUSTRIAL ADMINISTRATION

PRICE

**Dictionary of Industrial Administration**
Edited by J. Lee, C.B.E., M.A., M.Com.Sc. Two Vols. . . . . . . . . . . Net 63/-

**Employment Management**
Compiled and Edited by Daniel Bloomfield . Net 8/6

**Engineering Factory Supplies**
By W. J. Hiscox . . . . . . . . Net 5/-

**Factory Administration in Practice**
By W. J. Hiscox . . . . . . . . Net 8/6

**Factory Lay-Out, Planning and Progress**
By W. J. Hiscox . . . . . . . . Net 7/6

**Factory Organization**
By C. H. Northcott, M.A., Ph.D., O. Sheldon, B.A., J. W. Wardropper, B.Sc., B.Com., A.C.W.A., and L. Urwick, M.A. . . . . . . . . Net 7/6

**Fair Wage, A** By E. Batten . . . . Net 2/6

**Industrial Conflict**
By the Right Hon. George N. Barnes . Net 3/6

**Industrial Control (Applied to Manufacture)**
By F. M. Lawson, A.M.I.C.E., A.M.I.Mech.E. . Net 8/6

**Industrial Organization**
By John Lee, C.B.E., M.A., M.Com.Sc. . . Net 5/-

**Industrial Organization, The Evolution of**
By B. F. Shields, M.A. . . . . . Net 10/6

**Introduction to Industrial Administration, An**
By J. Lee, C.B.E., M.A., M.Com.Sc. . . Net 5/-

**Labour Organization**
By J. Cunnison, M.A. . . . . . . Net 7/6

**Lectures on Industrial Administration**
Edited by B. Muscio, M.A. . . . . . Net 6/-

**Letters to an Absentee Director**
By John Lee, C.B.E., M.A., M.Com.Sc. . . Net 5/-

**Management**
By J. Lee, C.B.E., M.A., M.Com.Sc. . . Net 5/-

**Modern Industrial Movements**
Edited by D. Bloomfield . . . . . Net 10/6

**New Leadership in Industry, The**
By S. A. Lewisohn . . . . . . Net 7/6

**Outlines of Industrial Administration**
By R. O. Herford, H. T. Hildage, and H. G. Jenkins . . . . . . . . Net 6/-

## Industrial Administration—contd.

PRICE

**Philosophy of Management, The**
By Oliver Sheldon, B.A. . . . . . Net 10/6

**Principles of Industrial Administration, An Introduction to**
By A. P. M. Fleming, C.B.E., M.Sc., M.I.E.E., and H. J. Brocklehurst, M.Eng., A.M.I.E.E. . Net 3/6

**Principles of Industrial Welfare**
By J. Lee, C.B.E., M.A., M.Com.Sc. . . . . Net 5/-

**Problems of Labour**
Compiled and Edited by Daniel Bloomfield . Net 8/6

**Research in Industry**
By A. P. M. Fleming, C.B.E., M.Sc., M.I.E.E., and J. G. Pearce, B.Sc., A.M.I.E.E. . . . Net 10/6

**Sharing Profits With Employees**
By J. A. Bowie, M.A. . . . . . . Net 10/6

**Time Standardization of Workshop Operations**
By T. Pilkington, M.I.Mech.E. . . . . Net 16/-

**Welfare Work in Industry**
Edited by E. T. Kelly . . . . . . Net 5/-

**Workshop Committees**
By C. G. Renold . . . . . . . Net 1/-

## BUSINESS ORGANIZATION AND MANAGEMENT

**Business Management**
By Percival White . . . . . . Net 15/-

**Clubs and Their Management**
By F. W. Pixley . . . . . . . Net 10/6

**Colliery Office Organization and Accounts**
By J. W. Innes, F.C.A., and T. C. Campbell, F.C.I. Net 7/6

**Commercial Management**
By C. L. Bolling . . . . . . . Net 10/6

**Counting-House and Factory Organization**
By J. Gilmour Williamson . . . . . Net 7/6

**Drapery Business Organization, Management and Accounts.** By J. Ernest Bayley . Net 7/6

**Filing Systems.** By E. A. Cope . . . . Net 3/6

**Flour Milling Industry, Organization and Management of the.** By E. L. Pearson. Net 12/6

PRICE

**Grocery Business Organization and Management.** By C. L. T. BEECHING, O.B.E., and J. A. SMART . . . . . . . . . Net 6/-

**Hire-Purchase Trading**
By CUNLIFFE L. BOLLING . . . . . Net 10/6

**Hotel Organization, Management, and Accountancy**
By G. DE BONI, Hotel Manager, and F. F. SHARLES, F.S.A.A., F.C.I.S. . . . . . . . Net 10/6

**How to Manage a Private Hotel**
By P. HOBBS . . . . . . . . Net 3/6

**How to Organize Bazaars, Concerts; Fêtes, Exhibitions, etc.**
By F. ATTFIELD FAWKES . . . . . Net 6/-

**Ironmongery and Ironmongers' Accounts**
By S. W. FRANCIS . . . . . . . Net 3/6

**Multiple Shop Organization**
By A. E. HAMMOND . . . . . . Net 6/-

**Office Machines, Appliances, and Methods**
By W. DESBOROUGH, F.C.I. . . . . . . Net 6/-

**Office Organization and Management, Including Secretarial Work**
By LAWRENCE R. DICKSEE, M.Com., F.C.A., and SIR H. E. BLAIN, C.B.E. . . . . . Net 7/6

**Organization of a Small Business, The**
By W. A. SMITH . . . . . . . . Net 2/6

**Self-Organization for Business Men**
By MORLEY DAINOW, B.Sc.(Hons.), Lond. . Net 5/-

**Solicitor's Office Organization, Management, and Accounts**
By E. A. COPE and H. W. H. ROBINS . . Net 6/-

**Stockbroker's Office, The**
By J. E. DAY . . . . . . . . Net 7/6

**Stores Accounts and Stores Control**
By J. H. BURTON . . . . . . . Net 5/-

## MUNICIPAL WORK

PRICE

**Local Government of the United Kingdom, and the Irish Free State The**
By J. J. Clarke, M.A., F.S.S. . . . . Net 12/6

**Municipal Accounting Systems**
By S. Whitehead, A.S.A.A., A.C.I.S. . . . Net 5/-

**Municipal Audit Programmes**
By the same Author . . . . . . Net 3/6

**Municipal Book-keeping**
By J. H. McCall, F.S.A.A. . . . . . Net 7/6

**Municipal and Local Government Law**
By H. E. Smith, LL.B. . . . . . . Net 10/6

**Municipal Organization**
By M. H. Cox, LL.B. . . . . . . Net 5/-

**Municipal Student's Examination Notebook**
By S. Whitehead, A.S.A.A., A.C.I.S. . . . Net 7/6

**Municipal Series**
Edited by William Bateson, A.C.A., F.S.A.A.
Describes the Organization and Administration in the Various Departments of a Municipality.

**Principles of Organization**
By W. Bateson, A.C.A., F.S.A.A. . . . Net 3/6

**Education Department**
By A. E. Ikin, B.Sc., LL.D. . . . . Net 7/6

**Electricity Undertaking**
By C. L. E. Stewart, M.I.E.E. . . . Net 6/-

**Finance Department**
By W. Bateson, A.C.A., F.S.A.A. . . . Net 7/6

**Gas Undertaking**
By E. Upton, F.S.A.A. . . . . . Net 5/-

**Municipal Engineer and Surveyor's Department.** By E. J. Elford . . . Net 10/6

**Public Health Department**
By W. A. Leonard . . . . . Net 6/-

**Rating Department**
By A. H. Peacock, M.A., A.S.A.A. . . . Net 5/-

**Town Clerk's Department and the Justices' Clerk's Department**
By A. S. Wright and E. H. Singleton . Net 7/6

**Tramways Department**
By S. B. N. Marsh . . . . . Net 6/-

**Waterworks Department**
By F. J. Alban, F.S.A.A., F.I.M.T.A., A.C.I.S. Net 10/6

## SALESMANSHIP

| | | PRICE |
|---|---|---|
| **Building Retail Sales.** By C. C. KNIGHTS . | Net | 5/- |
| **Commercial Travelling.** By A. E. BULL . | Net | 3/6 |
| **Craft of Silent Salesmanship**<br>By C. MAXWELL TREGURTHA and J. W. FRINGS | Net | 5/- |
| **Mail Order and Instalment Trading**<br>By A. E. BULL . . . . . . . | Net | 7/6 |
| **Mail Order Organization**<br>By P. E. WILSON . . . . . . . | Net | 3/6 |
| **Modern Sales Correspondence**<br>By D. M. WILSON . . . . . . . | Net | 5/- |
| **Outline of Sales Management, An**<br>By C. C. KNIGHTS, *Sales Consultant* . . | Net | 5/- |
| **Personal Salesmanship**<br>By R. SIMMAT, M.A. . . . . . . | Net | 5/- |
| **Practical Aids to Retail Selling**<br>By A. EDWARD HAMMOND . . . . | Net | 7/6 |
| **Practical Salesmanship**<br>By N. C. FOWLER, Junr. . . . . . | Net | 7/6 |
| **Principles of Retailing**<br>By N. A. BRISCO, Ph.D. . . . . . . | Net | 16/- |
| **Psychology as a Sales Factor**<br>By A. J. GREENLY . . . . . . . | Net | 10/6 |
| **Retail Salesmanship.** By C. L. BOLLING . | Net | 7/6 |
| **Sales Management.** By C. L. BOLLING . | Net | 10/6 |
| **Salesmanship**<br>By W. A. CORBION and G. E. GRIMSDALE . | Net | 3/6 |
| **Salesmanship**<br>By WILLIAM MAXWELL . . . . . . | Net | 5/- |
| **Salesmanship, Technique of**<br>By C. C. KNIGHTS . . . . . . . | Net | 5/- |
| **Shop Fittings and Display**<br>By A. E. HAMMOND . . . . . . | Net | 5/- |
| **Successful Retailing.** By E. N. SIMON . . | Net | 5/- |
| **Training for More Sales**<br>By C. C. KNIGHTS, *Sales Consultant* . . | Net | 5/- |
| **Training for Travelling Salesmen**<br>By F. W. SHRUBSALL . . . . . . | Net | 2/6 |

## TRANSPORT

| | | PRICE |
|---|---|---|
| **Canals and Inland Waterways** By GEORGE CADBURY and S. P. DOBBS, B.A. . | Net | 7/6 |
| **Commercial Air Transport** By LIEUT-COL. IVO EDWARDS, C.M.G., and F. TYMMS, M.C., A.F.R.Ae.S. . . . . . . . | Net | 7/6 |
| **History and Economics of Transport, The** By A. W. KIRKALDY, M.A., B.Litt., M.Com., and A. D. EVANS . . . . . . . | Net | 16/- |
| **Industrial Traffic Management** By G. B. LISSENDEN . . . . . . | Net | 25/- |
| **Modern Dock Operation** By D. ROSS-JOHNSON, C.B.E., V.D., M.Inst.I. . | Net | 6/- |
| **Modern Railway Operation** By D. R. LAMB, M.Inst.T. . . . . . | Net | 7/6 |
| **Motor Road Transport.** By J. PHILLIMORE . | Net | 10/6 |
| **Port Economics** By B. CUNNINGHAM, D.Sc., B.E., F.R.S.E., M.Inst.C.E. . . . . . . . . . | Net | 6/- |
| **Railway Electrification and Traffic Problems** By P. BURTT . . . . . . . . . | Net | 10/6 |
| **Railway Rates: Principles and Problems** By P. BURTT, M.Inst.T. . . . . . . . | Net | 6/- |
| **Railway Statistics: Their Compilation and Use.** By A. E. KIRKUS, O.B.E., M.Inst.T. . | Net | 5/- |
| **Rights and Duties of Transport Undertakings** By H. B. DAVIES, M.A. . . . . . . | Net | 5/- |
| **Road Making and Road Using** By T. SALKIELD, M.Inst.C.E., M.Inst.T. . . | Net | 7/6 |
| **Road Transport Operation—Passenger** By R. STUART PILCHER, F.R.S.E., M.Inst.T. . | Net | 10/6 |
| **Traders' Rail Charges Up to Date** By J. W. PARKER, A.M.Inst.T. . . . . | Net | 3/6 |
| **Transport Management, Practical** By ANDREW HASTIE . . . . . . . | Net | 10/6 |

## LAW

PRICE

**Bankruptcy, Deeds of Arrangement, etc.**
By W. VALENTINE BALL, M.A., *Barrister-at-Law* Net 12/6

**Bills, Cheques, and Notes**
By J. A. SLATER, B.A., LL.B. (Lond.). . . Net 6/-

**Business Tenant, The**
By EDWARD S. COX-SINCLAIR, and T. HYNES, . Net 7/6

**Commercial Law of England, The**
By J. A. SLATER, B.A., LL.B. (Lond.) . . Net 3/6

**Companies and Company Law**
By A. C. CONNELL, LL.B. (Lond.), revised by W. E. WILKINSON, LL.D. . . . . . . Net 6/-

**Company Case Law**
By F. D. HEAD, B.A. (Oxon) . . . . Net 7/6

**Company Law**
By D. F. DE L'HOSTE RANKING, M.A., LL.D., and ERNEST EVAN SPICER, F.C.A. . . . . Net 10/-

**Elements of Commercial Law, The**
By A. H. DOUGLAS, LL.B. (Lond.) . . . Net 2/-

**Elementary Law**
By E. A. COPE. Revised by H. COSWAY . . Net 4/-

**Examination Notes on Commercial Law**
By R. W. HOLLAND, O.B.E., M.A., M.Sc., LL.D. . Net 2/6

**Examination Notes on Company Law**
By R. W. HOLLAND, O.B.E., M.A., M.Sc., LL.D. . Net 2/6

**Executorship Law and Accounts**
By D. F. DE L'HOSTE RANKING, M.A., LL.D., E. E. SPICER, F.C.A., and E. C. PEGLER, F.C.A. Net 15/-

**Guide to Company Law**
By R. W. HOLLAND, O.B.E., M.A., M.Sc. LL.D. . Net 3/6

**Guide to Railway Law**
By ARTHUR E. CHAPMAN, M.A., LL.D. (Camb.) . Net 7/6

**Introduction to Commercial Law**
By NORMAN A. WEBB, B.Sc. . . . . . 5/-

**Law for Journalists**
By CHARLES PILLEY, *Barrister-at-Law* . . Net 5/-

**Law for the House-Owner**
By A. H. COSWAY . . . . . . . Net 2/6

**Law of Carriage by Railway, The. In Great Britain and Ireland**
By L. R. LIPSETT, M.A., LL.D., and T. J. D. ATKINSON, M.A. . . . . . . Net 50/-

PRICE

**Law of Contract, The**
By R. W. HOLLAND, O.B.E., M.A., M.Sc., LL.D. Net 5/–

**Law of Joint Stock Companies**
By W. J. WESTON, M.A., B.Sc., *of Gray's Inn, Barrister-at-Law* . . . . . . . . . Net 7/6

**Law of Master and Servant**
By F. R. BATT, LL.M. . . . . . . Net 10/6

**Law Relating to Building and Contracts**
By W. T. CRESWELL, *Barrister-at-Law* . . Net 12/6

**Legal Terms, Phrases, and Abbreviations**
By E. A. COPE . . . . . . . Net 3/–

**Mercantile Law**
By J. A. SLATER, B.A., LL.B. (Lond.) Revised by R. W. HOLLAND, O.B.E., M.A., M.Sc., LL.D., *of the Middle Temple* . . . . . . . Net 7/6

**Partnership Law and Accounts**
By R. W. HOLLAND, O.B.E., M.A., M.Sc., LL.D. Net 6/–

**Principles of Marine Law**
By LAWRENCE DUCKWORTH . . . . . Net 7/6

**Questions and Answers on Commercial Law**
By R. W. HOLLAND, O.B.E., M.A., M.Sc., LL.D. Net 5/–

**Questions and Answers on Company Law**
By G. WILLIAM FORTUNE, F.S.A.A., F.C.I.S. (Hons.), and D. R. MATHESON, M.A. (Hons.), A.S.A.A. (Hons.) Net 5/–

**Railway Act, 1921, The**
By R. P. GRIFFITHS, F.C.I., F.B.E.A., Grad.Inst.T. Net 2/6

**Rights and Duties of Liquidators, Trustees, and Receivers, The**
By D. F. DE L'HOSTE RANKING, M.A., LL.D., ERNEST E. SPICER, F.C.A., and ERNEST C. PEGLER, F.C.A. Net 15/–

**Solicitor's Clerk's Guide.** By E. A. COPE . Net 4/–

**Trade Mark Law and Practice**
By A. W. GRIFFITHS, B.Sc. (Eng.), Lond. . Net 10/6

**Trusts: Law, Administration, and Accounts**
By C. KELLY and J. COLE-HAMILTON . . Net 15/–

**Wills, Executors, and Trustees**
By R. W. HOLLAND, O.B.E., M.A., M.Sc., LL.D. Net 2/6

## REFERENCE BOOKS

| | | PRICE |
|---|---|---|
| **Bedrock of Modern Business, The** | | |
| By James Stephenson, M.A., M.Com., D.Sc. . | Net | 15/- |
| **Business Building** | | |
| Edited by F. F. Sharles, F.S.A.A., F.C.I.S. 2 Vols. | Net | 42/- |
| **Business Cycles. The Problem and Its Setting** | | |
| By W. C. Mitchell . . . . . . | Net | 30/- |
| **Business Forecasting and Its Practical Application.** By W. Wallace, M.Com. (Lond.) . | Net | 7/6 |
| **Business Man's Encyclopaedia and Dictionary of Commerce** | | |
| Edited by Frank Heywood, F.C.I.S. Two Vols. | Net | 47/6 |
| **Business Man's Guide** | | |
| Edited by J. A. Slater, B.A., LL.B. . . | Net | 6/- |
| **Business Statistics** | | |
| By R. W. Holland, O.B.E., M.A., M.Sc., LL.D. | Net | 3/6 |
| **Business Terms, Phrases, etc.** . . | Net | 3/6 |
| **Buying and Selling a Business** | | |
| By A. H. Cosway . . . . . . . | Net | 3/6 |
| **Cable and Wireless Communications of the World, The** | | |
| By F. J. Brown, C.B., C.B.E., M.A., B.Sc. . | Net | 7/6 |
| **Charting, Manual of** . . . . . . | Net | 6/- |
| **Charts and Graphs** | | |
| By Karl G. Karsten, B.A. (Oxon) . . | Net | 25/- |
| **Commercial Arbitrations** | | |
| By E. J. Parry, B.Sc., F.I.C., F.C.S. . . | Net | 3/6 |
| **Commercial Commodities** | | |
| By F. Matthews, B.Sc., A.I.C., F.C.S. . . | Net | 12/6 |
| **Commercial Contracts.** By E. J. Parry . | Net | 5/- |
| **Commercial Self-Educator** | | |
| Edited by R. W. Holland, O.B.E., M.A., M.Sc., LL.D. Two Vols. . . . . . . . . | Net | 30/- |
| **Commodities of Commerce** | | |
| By J. A. Slater, B.A., LL.B. . . . . | Net | 6/- |
| **Cotton World, The** | | |
| Compiled and Edited by J. A. Todd, M.A., B.L. . | Net | 5/- |
| **Dictionary of the World's Commercial Products** | | |
| By J. A. Slater, B.A., LL.B. (Lond.) . . | Net | 5/- |

## Reference Books—contd.

| | | PRICE |
|---|---|---|
| **Discount, Commission, and Brokerage Tables** By ERNEST HEAVINGHAM | Net | 1/6 |
| **Guide to the Improvement of the Memory** By the late REV. J. H. BACON | Net | 1/6 |
| **Handbook on Wills, A.** By A. H. COSWAY | Net | 2/6 |
| **How to Collect Accounts by Letter** By C. HANNEFORD-SMITH | Net | 3/6 |
| **How to Grant Credit** By CUTHBERT GREIG | Net | 3/6 |
| **History, Law, and Practice of the Stock Exchange, The.** By A. P. POLEY, B.A. | Net | 7/6 |
| **Investment Principles and Practices** By R. E. BADGER, Ph.D. | Net | 21/- |
| **Investor's Manual, The** By W. W. WALL, F.S.S., F.J.I. | Net | 3/6 |
| **Mercantile Terms and Abbreviations** | Net | 1/6 |
| **Money and the Stock and Share Markets, The** By EMIL DAVIES | Net | 2/- |
| **Money Making in Stocks and Shares** By SYDNEY A. MOSELEY | Net | 7/6 |
| **Public Speaking, Essentials of** By W. C. DUBOIS, A.M., LL.B. | Net | 8/6 |
| **Raw Materials of Commerce** In 2 vols. Edited by J. H. VANSTONE, F.R.G.S. | Net | 40/- |
| **Report Writing** By CARL G. GAUM, M.E., and HAROLD F. GRAVES, M.A. | Net | 12/6 |
| **Romance of World Trade, The** By A. P. DENNIS, Ph.D., LL.D. | Net | 15/- |
| **Shareholder's Manual, The** By H. H. BASSETT | Net | 3/6 |
| **Speak in Public, How to** By C. F. CARR and F. E. STEVENS | Net | 3/6 |
| **Statistics** By WILLIAM VERNON LOVITT, Ph.D., and HENRY F. HOLTZCLAW, Ph.D. | Net | 15/- |
| **Statistics and Their Application to Commerce** By A. L. BODDINGTON | Net | 12/6 |
| **Types of Business Enterprise** By M. C. CROSS, LL.B., Ph.D. | Net | 21/- |

## FOREIGN LANGUAGES

### FRENCH

| | | PRICE |
|---|---|---|
| **Progressive French Grammar**<br>By Dr. F. A. Hedgcock, M.A., D.ès.L. | Net | 5/6 |
| **Commercial French Grammar**<br>By F. W. M. Draper, M.A., B. ès. L. | Net | 2/6 |
| **French-English and English-French Commercial Dictionary**<br>By F. W. Smith | Net | 7/6 |
| **Manual of French Commercial Correspondence**<br>By G. W. Macdonald | Net | 5/- |
| **Correct French Speech**<br>By B. Dumville, M.A., F.C.P. | | 1/6 |

### GERMAN

| | | |
|---|---|---|
| **A New German Grammar**<br>By J. Keegan, M.A. | Net | 5/- |
| **Commercial German Grammar**<br>By J. Bithell, M.A. | Net | 3/6 |
| **A New German-English and English-German Dictionary for General Use**<br>By F. C. Hebert and L. Hirsch | Net | 15/- |
| **German-English and English-German Commercial Dictionary**<br>By J. Bithell, M.A. | Net | 16/- |
| **Commercial Correspondence in German.** | Net | 3/6 |

### SPANISH

| | | |
|---|---|---|
| **Spanish Commercial Grammar**<br>By C. A. Toledano | Net | 4/6 |
| **Spanish-English and English-Spanish Commercial Dictionary**<br>By G. R. Macdonald | Net | 12/6 |
| **Manual of Spanish Commercial Correspondence**<br>By G. R. Macdonald | Net | 4/6 |

## ITALIAN

PRICE

**Baretti's Italian and English Dictionary**
Compiled by GUGLIELMO COMELATI and J. DAVENPORT. In two volumes (Reprinted) . . . . . Net 25/-

**Italian Commercial Grammar**
By LUIGI RICCI . . . . . . . . Net 4/-

**Italian-English and English-Italian Commercial Dictionary**
By G. R. MACDONALD. . . . . . . Net 30/-

**Mercantile Correspondence, English-Italian**
Net 5/-

## PORTUGUESE

**Portuguese-English and English-Portuguese Commercial Dictionary**
By F. W. SMITH . . . . . . . Net 16/-

**Mercantile Correspondence, English-Portuguese.** . . . . . . . . . Net 3/6

## PITMAN'S SHORTHAND

For Complete List of Textbooks, Phrase Books, Dictation Books, Reading Books, etc., see Pitman's "SHORTHAND AND TYPEWRITING CATALOGUE."

**Pitman's Shorthand Instructor** . . . . 4/6

**Pitman's Shorthand Commercial Course** . 4/6

**Pitman's Shorthand Rapid Course** . . . 4/6

**Shorter Course in Pitman's Shorthand** . 1/-

**Shorthand Dictionary** . . . . . . . . 7/6

**English and Shorthand Dictionary** . . . 10/-

**Shorthand Clerk's Guide**
By V. E. COLLINGE, A.C.I.S. . . . . . . 2/6

**Progressive Dictator** . . . . . . . . 2/6

**Phonographic Phrase Book** . Paper 1/6, Cloth 2/-

## TYPEWRITING

| | | PRICE |
|---|---|---|
| **Pitman's Commercial Typewriting**<br>By W. and E. WALMSLEY | | 5/- |
| **Pitman's Typewriter Manual** | | 6/- |
| **Business Typewriting**<br>By F. HEELIS, F.C.I.S. | | 2/- |
| **Advanced Typewriting**<br>By the same Author | | 3/6 |
| **Typist's Companion, The**<br>By MAXWELL CROOKS, F.Inc.T.T., F.I.P.S. | Net | 2/- |
| **Touch Typewriting for Teachers**<br>By MAXWELL CROOKS, F.Inc.T.T., F.I.P.S., F.C.T.S. (Inc.) | Net | 7/6 |
| **Touch Typewriting Exercises**<br>By T. J. SIMONS, F.C.T.S., F.I.P.S. | | 1/6 |
| **Practical Course in Touch Typewriting**<br>By C. E. SMITH | | 2/- |
| **Dictionary of Typewriting**<br>By H. ETHERIDGE | Net | 7/6 |
| **Questions and Answers on Typewriting and Office Procedure**<br>By ARTHUR E. MORTON | | 7/6 |
| **Royal Society of Arts Typewriting Tests**<br>By A. E. MORTON. No. 1, Elementary; No. 2, Intermediate; No. 3, Advanced. Each | | 2/6 |
| **Mechanical Devices of the Typewriter**<br>By R. T. NICHOLSON, M.A. | Net | 6/- |
| **Modern Typewriting and Manual of Office Procedure**<br>By A. E. MORTON | | 5/6 |
| **Work and Management of a Copying Office, The**<br>By G. C. MENZIES | Net | 10/6 |
| **Pitman's Gramophone Method of Rhythmic Typewriting**<br>Comprises a complete set of specially arranged gramophone records for use in the Touch Typewriting Class and a series of carefully graded keyboard exercises | Net | 35/- |
| Exercises only | Each | 1/6 |

*Complete List post free on application.*

# COMMON COMMODITIES AND INDUSTRIES

Each book in crown 8vo, illustrated. **3s.** net.

In each of the handbooks in this series a particular product or industry is treated by an expert writer and practical man of business. Beginning with the life history of the plant, or other natural product, he follows its development until it becomes a commercial commodity, and so on through the various phases of its sale in the market and its purchase by the consumer.

**Acids, Alkalis, and Salts.** (Adlam.)

**Alcohol in Commerce and Industry.** (Simmonds.)

**Aluminium.** (Mortimer.)

**Anthracite.** (Summers.)

**Asbestos.** (Summers.)

**Bookbinding Craft and Industry.** (Harrison.)

**Books—From the MS. to the Bookseller.** (Young.)

**Boot and Shoe Industry, The.** (Harding.)

**Bread and Bread Baking.** (Stewart.)

**Brushmaker, The.** (Kiddier.)

**Butter and Cheese.** (Tisdale and Jones.)

**Button Industry, The.** (Jones.)

**Carpets.** (Brinton.)

**Clays and Clay Products.** (Searle.)

**Clocks and Watches.** (Overton.)

**Clothing Industry, The.** (Poole.)

**Cloths and the Cloth Trade.** (Hunter.)

**Coal.** (Wilson.)

**Coal Tar.** (Warnes.)

**Coffee—From Grower to Consumer.** (Keable.)

**Cold Storage and Ice Making.** (Springett.)

**Concrete and Reinforced Concrete.** (Twelvetrees.)

**Copper—From the Ore to the Metal.** (Picard.)

**Cordage and Cordage Hemp and Fibres.** (Woodhouse and Kilgour.)

**Corn Trade, The British.** (Barker.)

**Cotton.** (Peake.)

**Cotton Spinning.** (Wade.)

**Cycle Industry, The.** (Grew.)

**Drugs in Commerce.** (Humphrey.)

**Dyes.** (Hall.)

**Electric Lamp Industry, The.** (Percival.)

**Electricity.** (Neale.)

**Engraving.** (Lascelles.)

**Explosives, Modern.** (Levy.)

**Fertilizers.** (Cave.)

**Film Industry, The.** (Boughey.)

**Fishing Industry, The.** (Gibbs.)

**Furniture.** (Binstead.)

**Furs and the Fur Trade.** (Sachs.)

**Gas and Gas Making.** (Webber.)

**Glass and Glass Making.** (Marson.)

**Gloves and the Glove Trade.** (Ellis.)

**Gold.** (White.)

**Gums and Resins.** (Parry.)

**Incandescent Lighting.** (Levy.)

**Ink.** (Mitchell.)

**Iron and Steel.** (Hood.)

**Ironfounding.** (Whiteley.)

**Jute Industry, The.** (Woodhouse and Kilgour.)

**Knitted Fabrics.** (Chamberlain and Quilter.)

**Lead, including Lead Pigments.** (Smythe.)

**Leather.** (Adcock.)

**Linen.** (Moore.)

**Locks and Lock Making.** (Butter.)

**Match Industry, The.** (Dixon.)

**Meat Industry, The.** (Wood.)

## Common Commodities and Industries—contd.

**Motor Industry, The.** (WYATT.)
**Nickel.** (WHITE.)
**Oil Power.** (NORTH.)
**Oils.** (MITCHELL.)
**Paints and Varnishes.** (JENNINGS.)
**Paper.** (MADDOX.)
**Patent, Smokeless, and Semi-Smokeless Fuels.** (GREENE and PERKIN.)
**Perfumery, The Raw Materials of.** (PARRY.)
**Photography.** (GAMBLE.)
**Platinum Metals, The.** (SMITH.)
**Player Piano, The.** (WILSON.)
**Pottery.** (NOKE and PLANT.)
**Rice.** (DOUGLAS.)
**Rubber.** (STEVENS and STEVENS.)
**Salt.** (CALVERT.)
**Shipbuilding and the Shipbuilding Industry.** (MITCHELL.)
**Silk.** (HOOPER.)
**Silver.** (WHITE.)
**Soap.** (SIMMONS.)
**Sponges.** (CRESSWELL.)
**Starch and Starch Products.** (AUDEN.)
**Stones and Quarries.** (HOWE.)
**Straw Hats.** (INWARDS.)
**Sugar.** (MARTINEAU.) (Revised by EASTICK.)
**Sulphur and Allied Products.** (AUDEN.)
**Talking Machines.** (MITCHELL.)
**Tea.** (IBBETSON.)
**Telegraphy, Telephony, and Wireless.** (POOLE.)
**Textile Bleaching.** (STEVEN.)
**Timber.** (BULLOCK.)
**Tin and the Tin Industry.** (MUNDEY.)
**Tobacco.** (TANNER.) (Revised by DREW).
**Velvet and the Corduroy Industry.** (COOKE.)
**Wall Paper.** (WARD.)
**Weaving.** (CRANKSHAW.)
**Wheat and Its Products.** (MILLAR.)
**Wine and the Wine Trade.** (SIMON.)
**Wool.** (HUNTER.)
**Worsted Industry, The.** (DUMVILLE and KERSHAW.)
**Zinc and Its Alloys.** (LONES.)

## Technical Dictionary of Engineering and Industrial Science in Seven Languages: English, French, Spanish, Italian, Portuguese, Russian, and German.

In four volumes, each in crown 4to, buckram gilt, 2230 pp. £8 8s. net, complete.

Compiled by ERNEST SLATER, M.I.E.E., M.I.Mech.E., in collaboration with leading Authorities.

## PITMAN'S SHORTHAND

**Invaluable to all Business and Professional Men**

**Sir Isaac Pitman & Sons, Ltd., Parker Street, Kingsway, London, W.C.2**

PRINTED IN GREAT BRITAIN AT THE PITMAN PRESS, BATH
(9811W)